The Sir Misha Black Medal

Designed by Malcolm Garrett RDI
Project management Wilhelmina Bunn
Copy editor Kasper de Graaf
Production assistant Alice Magagnin
Printed in England by Galloway's
on G . F Smith Munken Lynx Smooth Natural White

Published and distributed by Design Manchester / Eyewear Publishing

**Design
Manchester**   EYEWEAR PUBLISHING   G . F
—   SMITH
                                                 1885 ONWARDS

www.mishablackawards.org.uk
www.designmcr.com
www.eyewearpublishing.com

ISBN 978-1-912477-80-7

Fitness For What Purpose?

THE · SIR MISHA BLACK AWARDS

40

1978–2018

Essays on design education celebrating
40 years of the Sir Misha Black Awards

Edited by Mary V Mullin and Sir Christopher Frayling
Foreword by HRH The Prince Philip, Duke of Edinburgh

Contents

Preface

The Royal Commission for the Exhibition of 1851 provides fellowships and grants for top level science and industrial research and industrial design students. Some 30 awards are made each year which, together with a number of special grants, exceed £3.5m in value.

Originally set up to stage the Great Exhibition, the Royal Commission was kept in being to invest the Exhibition's substantial profit. It first acquired the site in South Kensington on which the three great museums, the Royal Albert Hall, Imperial College and the Royal Colleges of Art and Music now stand, and it continues to own and manage the freehold of much of this estate. When the development of the estate was largely complete, in 1891, the Commission then began an education and research awards programme which it continues to grow to this day.

The Sir Misha Black Awards Committee acknowledges with much gratitude the generous support of the Royal Commission for the Exhibition of 1851 which has made this publication possible.

Foreword

HRH Prince Philip presents the first Sir Misha Black Medal at Buckingham Palace in 1978.

Left to right: HRH Prince Philip, Sir William Coldstream (recipient of the Medal), Milner Grey (Chairman, SIAD Trustee Board), Leslie Julius (MD, Hille Furniture), Richard Negus (President, SIAD), Geoffrey Adams (Secretary, SIAD).

This year is the 40th anniversary of the inauguration of the Sir Misha Black Medal for distinguished services to Design Education, awarded in memory of a man who was a pioneer in the teaching and practice of industrial design, and who played a crucial role in the development of design from the 1950s to the 1970s. I presided over the first of these awards in 1978, which took place at Buckingham Palace, when the recipient was Sir William Coldstream, and I am pleased to have been associated with them ever since.

Their aim is to acknowledge the important contribution of the individuals to the teaching of design at all levels, from anywhere in the world – as designers, as champions, as mentors and as educators.

The contributions of such individuals are still not adequately valued. They have demonstrated, through their examples, how design can create value out of technology, how design can energise industry, and how design can be a very satisfying career.

This book tells the forty year story of the Sir Misha Black Awards, and of the achievements to which they have drawn much-needed attention.

Introduction

Portrait of Sir Misha Black by Carel Weight, 1975.

The Misha as Before

Professor Sir Christopher Frayling
College of Medallists

In the heroic old days, the portrait would have shown a skull resting on some leather-bound books, or some basic geometrical instruments, or a quill pen and goatskin parchment – and the subject, head-on-hand in a 'think' pose, would have been wearing a long, flowing robe made of heavy damask known as a 'banyan'. The setting would have been suitably gloomy and autumnal. That's how thinkers and designers were expected to be seen.

But in Carel Weight's 1975 portrait of Sir Misha Black, the setting is more upbeat – patterned red curtains – and the subject, instead of head-on-hand, seems to be having a genial chat, with a French cigarette in his mouth. He is wearing a suit rather than a damask robe. And gone are the traditional signifiers of intellect and *disegno*, to make way for a pile of committee papers on his lap…

Were these papers perhaps generated by one of the numerous fledgling design organisations with which Misha was busily associated – the International Council of Societies of Industrial Design (ICSID), which he helped to found in 1955, realising that the language of design crossed national boundaries; or the Society of Industrial Artists and Designers (member, 1932–77; President, 1954–56); or the Council of Industrial Design – precursor of today's Design Council (member, 1955–64); or the Royal Designers for Industry (Faculty, 1957–77; Master, 1973–74); or the Society for Education in Art/National Advisory Council for Art Education (1942–59; 1959–72)…or the Board of the British Museum, the Science Museum or the Institute of Contemporary Art… or…

Misha Black was certainly at the heart of the design infrastructure in Britain and overseas, at a time when it was in the process of defining itself, and a colleague has said of the hours and hours he spent on these committees, 'he was always *professional* in the best sense… and always believed in the value of design uplifting the quality of life'. He remembered seeing the words 'God Design' written over a conference doorway – which even he thought might be overdoing it – before realising it was Danish for 'good design'. I once fantasised, with the writer J.G. Ballard, about a science fiction story in which a man turns into a committee meeting. In my case, at the time, the transformation had – we thought – reached my knees. In Misha Black's case, it would have reached his chin – at the very least. And he was a prolific *designer* and *teacher* at the same time.

Those papers could have been to do with the day-to-day organisation of the Design Research Unit (DRU), the prototype design partnership bringing together a range of skills for all seasons, which he co-founded with Milner Gray just after the Second World War (1946), in the heady days of 'Britain Can Make It'. The centrepiece of that famously popular exhibition, at the Victoria & Albert Museum, was a section on 'the birth of an egg-cup' – the equivalent of Adam Smith's case-study of the pin factory – and Misha designed that as well. Today, partnerships on the DRU model are among the most likely of all destinations for design graduates in the UK. Or to do with the Festival of Britain in 1951, the tonic to the nation after the austerity of war which domesticated Modernism in design and architecture and which Misha Black coordinated (the Upstream elements)

with Hugh Casson: his role, an exceptionally demanding one, was to make sure that
the Festival – which involved all manner of jostling architects and designers of different
shades of opinionatedness – retained some kind of conceptual unity and integrity.
One of these designers recalled, 'he was at his best when things were going wrong'.
Misha Black's long experience in exhibition design (going back all the way to the Paris
International Exposition of 1937, the *Peace Pavilion*, the MARS exhibition of Modern
Architecture a year later, the British Pavilion at the New York World's Fair in 1939 and
his touring display-work for the Ministry of Information during the war) commanded a lot
of respect in the sector: architects and designers paid attention to him because of what
he had done as well as what he said. The Festival was mounted in double-quick time –
Hugh Casson reckoned this had something to do with the habit of 'command and obey'
which lingered after 1939–45 – but it still generated a lot of bureaucracy. As if that was
not enough, Misha Black helped to design the Dome of Discovery on London's South
Bank as well – with overall responsibility for the interior: he had to evaluate and edit
the many suggestions from the ten 'theme convenors' who were arguing with him and
amongst themselves about what should be exhibited inside, while passionately promoting
their special interests.

Possibly those papers were about the details of Misha Black's many public commissions
as a design consultant for London Transport (the Victoria Line on the underground),
the British Railways Board, British Overseas Airways Corporation and British European
Airways, the Post Office, the Gas Light and Coke company and London Zoo (the small
mammal house) – or his private commissions for Beagle aircraft, Vickers Ltd, Mather and
Platt machinery, the interior of the white-hulled *SS Oriana* – the last of the Orient Line's
great ocean liners, recently celebrated at the V&A – the offices of *The Times*… and many
other examples from his prodigious output, at a time when the manufacturing industry
was only just beginning to appreciate the value of design to its continued health.

Or – perhaps the most likely explanation, since Carel Weight was Professor of Painting
at the RCA at the same time as Misha Black was the College's first-ever Professor of
Industrial Design, and they both knew only too well how much paperwork and how many
meetings even a small-scale face-to-face postgraduate educational institution could
generate – the documents on Misha's lap concerned academic administration; or reports
about the resources needed to run the new 'Industrial Design Engineering' department
which had until recently – in the era before branding – been known a little more
prosaically as first 'Light Engineering and Furniture', then 'Wood, Metal and Plastics'.
1975, the year Weight's painting was made, was the year Misha Black retired from the
College as Professor Emeritus. He had occupied the Chair since 1959, and came to
see the value of teaching design in an art environment and art in a design environment –
provided 'the practicalities' (as he called them) and the customers were never forgotten.
During his tenure – this was and is unusual – he published many of his lectures, papers
and reflections in magazines and journals, a provocative selection of which were issued
in *The Black Papers on Design* in 1983, six years after his death. Over twenty of the
articles in his archive – post-1964 – were about design education at secondary and
tertiary levels. His subjects seem in many cases to be as timely now as they were then:
the limitations of design theory (or 'the methodological approach') for practitioners unless
it relates to the 'project in hand'; the positioning of industrial design somewhere on the
spectrum between 'aesthetics' and 'problem-solving'; the public perception of design
as mere 'styling' or 'dressed-up engineering'; the defining importance of 'the consumer
experience' (today known as 'user-centred design') and the danger of the 'measure of

man' approach which led inexorably to 'one size fits all' (more recently dubbed 'Nietzsche marketing'); the implications for designers and craftspeople of the move towards neo-conceptualism (or, as we now know it, de-materialisation) in Fine Art, and the continuing importance of *making* – of understanding materials – even in modern design teaching ('a period of handwork is, I believe, essential to the development of all designers'); the need to treat computers as *tools*, and to avoid being bedazzled by them – 'they should be relegated to commonplace acceptance'; design as the hyphen between science, technology and engineering – one of the reasons why a joint course between Imperial College and the Royal College of Art seemed to him an excellent idea. Are we spending too much time arguing about the aesthetic merits of this or that cup and saucer or piece of electrical equipment – or, come to that, egg-cup – when we should be devoting more of our intellectual energies to wider social and environmental issues? He much preferred the phrase 'design for people' to either of the mantras 'design for profit' *or* 'design for need'. The Royal Charter of the Royal College of Art, granted in 1967, stressed the importance of design to industry and economic development – but also, and equally, to 'social developments'; there was much ground to make up. Another question he liked asking: in place of the moral and visual certainties of Bauhaus Modernism, what do we have today and who is articulating it – 'they are now only partially valid'. What if the Modernists had confused a *style* with a set of external verities – a style which was right for its time, a suitable style for an age of austerity? What then? More specifically, and locally, should a Council of Industrial Design, or its successor Design Council, even attempt to be a Ministry of Taste – telling the public what was good for them – or had that approach become rather patronising? And if, in the Edwardian era, Fine Art had become the unofficial heart of the RCA curriculum… where should that heart reside in the second half of the twentieth century? Misha Black was thoughtful, compassionate – and good-humoured – in expressing his views, and evidently felt he had a responsibility by virtue of his position to do so publicly. In Victorian times, the designers of the day – and especially those who had some experience in education, from Christopher Dresser to Walter Crane and beyond – had been the pace-setters of public debate about design, circulating their lectures and articles and textbooks as widely as possible, and taking part in the resulting controversies: since then, the baton had passed, with one or two exceptions, to bureaucrats, curators and pundits. *The Black Papers* remain a benchmark, give or take a few out-of-date references, partly because Misha Black was that rare phenomenon – a design practitioner who enjoyed writing about things and organising things, and was gifted at both. He also had a well-stocked repertoire of pithy quotations.

In early July 1968, Misha Black became an Honorary Doctor of the Royal College of Art at the annual Convocation ceremony – only a year after the College had become a chartered university institution able to award its own degrees of MA and MDes. 1968 was proving to be a turbulent year for design in the UK: the lessons from the West Coast of America were being absorbed by the up-and-coming generation of artist-craftspeople, which scared the more traditional arts-and-crafts people mightily; the tweedy Council of Industrial Design, with its Cotswold Modernist bias, was struggling to come to terms with the vulgarity of Pop; the transition in colleges from technical training to university-equivalent education (NDD to Dip. AD) was proving traumatic in some quarters; *'les évènements'* of early May 1968 in Paris were beginning to have more impact on art schools than mainstream universities: a Roneo'ed student paper dared to question the status of architects and designers as 'experts'; a Guards officer went into the RCA's Senior Common Room, thinking it must be something to do with Basil Spence's new Knightsbridge Barracks (then under construction), and only realised his mistake when he tried to pay the bill; the Rector of the College Robin Darwin said that every evening he recited to himself the opening words of the *Nunc Dimittis*: 'Lord, now lettest thou thy servant depart in peace.' Many 1960s art students, he observed, 'had chips on their shoulders the size of epaulettes': the image, as well as the sentiment, said much about the attitudes of the powers-that-were in art education. There had been a large anti-Vietnam demonstration in Grosvenor Square in mid-March 1968 – involving a number of RCA students – and 'Black Power' was a topical catchphrase.

The Convocation ceremony took place in the Gulbenkian Hall, Kensington Gore (built 1961), beneath a large coloured lino-cut of the Lion and Unicorn designed by Edward Bawden and rescued from the Brussels World's Fair of 1958 – with Guards trumpeters in attendance for the fanfare, embroidered designer-robes with lots of glitter for the Rectorate, and a Silver College Yardstick (phoenix at the top, dodo at the bottom) – a world away from all the turbulence going on outside. The Lion, it was said, represented Solidity and Strength; the Unicorn represented creative imagination. *Design* magazine had recently noted:

> To the students there is a yawning gap between the conditions of their own lives in Earl's Court or Notting Hill and the quasi-traditional trappings which surround the Convocation ceremony...

The trappings, the pageantry and the heraldry, the article reminded its readers, were only *one year old*. The Lion was evidently in the ascendant.

The oration for Misha Black was written and delivered, in inimitably puckish style, by Christopher Cornford, a distant relative of the Darwin clan:

> Members of the Design Research Unit claim that their founder member and senior partner once received an envelope to 'Bishop Black, Divine Research Unit'. There was perhaps more aptness in this than the writer knew, for if bishops are, as we may hope, models of kindness, resolution, public spirit, clarity of intellect and unflagging energy, then Misha Black certainly qualifies to sit at the top end of their Bench. Whenever, throughout the world, designers, architects or industrialists are assembled together with creative intent, his alert and upright presence is the best possible guarantee of unanimity and effective outcome. In the realm of education, too, the Black Hand has been an unerring pointer towards progress in the training of designers, and the expansion of research: it is a Hand, moreover, that obeys a designer's and an architect's imagination, ceaselessly active in solving formal and functional problems of an amazing variety of artefacts, ranging in size from airports, liners and locomotives, down to the finest details of, say, hospital equipment. Countless honours and responsibilities have descended upon him in consequence: Black Power, at least in the international design world, is already a reality. There can be no better prescription for the future health of that world than *The Misha As Before*.

It was in this extraordinary man's name that the medals, and later the awards, were instituted, a year after his untimely death at the age of 67 – to celebrate outstanding achievement in design education. Misha Black's career had, after all, proved to be a milestone in the history of industrial design, its promotion and its teaching. The first-ever award, of a large medal with Misha's likeness and an inscription on it – designed by Michael Rizzello ARCA, lettering supervised by Milner Grey – was given to Sir William Coldstream for his important contribution to the restructuring of art and design education. Sir William had jointly chaired the committee of inquiry which concluded that art and design education should be considered not merely as professional training towards a vocation but should be treated as an alternative form of higher education in its own right. Up until the early 1960s, young artists and designers had been treated as second-class citizens in further and higher education, admitted by the tradesman's entrance: now, design could be seen as a valid intellectual as well as practical activity, something for which Misha Black had himself been arguing since the early 1960s. The ceremony took place at Buckingham Palace on 6th December 1978, and HRH the Duke of Edinburgh presented the first medal. Since then, he has kept in close touch with developments – and he presented mine, at the Medal's 25th anniversary. We are very grateful to him for contributing the *Foreword* to this volume.

It marks the 40th anniversary of the Misha Black Awards, another milestone. The Awards, which have helped to keep his name and his values in the public eye, have now lasted longer than Misha's own career as a designer and teacher. They remain unique in the field of design education – in its broadest sense – and have represented an opportunity to shine a spotlight into places which normally generate more heat than light. It seems timely to reflect on the changes which have happened, in his areas of interest, since the 1970s – among them, design at a time of increasing globalisation; the rise of design management and service design; changes in the definition of the word 'product' from 'a thing manufactured, made or assembled' to 'a bundle of services' as well; the changing public perception of design through colourful lifestyle pages and early-evening television; the evolving role of designers from being individual authors to becoming facilitators of change; the restructuring of polytechnics and colleges as universities – with their new emphasis on research into and through design; the changing social significance of the crafts from artist-craftspeople and designer-makers to the wider 'crafting' movement; the rhetoric of the 'creative industries' debate; from design for industry to design for people – 'the other 99%' – plus, of course, the implications for design teaching of digital technology and the rise of social media. The contributors to this volume – Medallists and Award recipients – reflect on some of these changes, from the perspectives of design practitioners and educators.

We have decided to present these short essays in three categories, matching Misha Black's main interests – the International picture; considerations for Design Education, and future developments within the Design Profession itself. Each of these categories is introduced by two of Misha Black's articles, to set the scene.

One area is not covered by these contributions – and it was a subject with which Misha Black was very concerned – and that is design education in secondary schools. He often alluded to premature selection into 'scientific and humanistic specialists', which meant that the foundations for design education (aesthetics plus engineering) were difficult to arrange. Where general education was concerned, he reckoned that 'creativity is not only the concern of those who practise the fine and the useful arts'. It belongs to everyone, whatever subject they happen to be studying. At the same time, he seems to have viewed design as a third culture, alongside science and the humanities. Misha Black once gave a televised talk to schools called 'Saucepans and Mammals'.

Design in schools – whether across the curriculum, or as a specialist subject – has been a hotly contested area in the decades since his time as a Professor. In General Education, 1988 – eleven years after his death, the year when the pioneering commentator on 'the machine age' Reyner Banham was awarded the medal – was the year when the Educational Reform Act made Britain the first country in the world to introduce by law mandatory Design and Technology (D&T) exams for all 16-year-olds. It looked as though the academic arguments – and the specialised research – about the benefits of D&T in secondary schools had at last been accepted by the establishment: arguments about design as an intellectual/practical subject in its own right, as a way of thinking about, and approaching, other academic subjects and as a source of rich vocational possibilities. D&T had, it seemed, shaken off its late-Victorian associations with Mr Chippy in the woodwork room and with low-attaining students who had trouble coping with words and numbers – shaken it off among teachers, learners, teacher-educators, school governors, politicians and interested parents. Design had achieved 'parity of esteem' with the other core disciplines (in the phrase of the time) rather than being taught in the outhouse.

The focus of the argument might change – from 'problem-solving', 'critical evaluation' via 'learning through doing', 'the iterative process' to 'the creative industries' – and the discipline might seem to be in a constant state of self-analysis which to the uncharitable resembled navel-gazing – but this was from a position of well-earned confidence and strength. When, in the mid-1990s, just after the 'Design and Make' reforms to the curriculum, 'the creative industries' argument was added to the mix, it gave design extra visibility as a key driver of economic success. This was a particularly effective argument in its day. I was involved, in the early part of this century, as Chair of the Design Council and Rector of the Royal College of Art, in trying hard to establish design as the silent partner in STEM. And for a moment it looked as though this might actually happen: a senior government minister actually said to me in 2009 that he thought it already had happened.

And then the tide turned. Misha Black was aware – in his various comments on the subject – of how fragile the arguments could be, and he was right. 'The creative industries' dropped from public discourse, to make way for 'productive industry'. Design was not included among the 'priority subjects' in the Browne Review of Higher Education – a serious setback for art and design colleagues and faculties. The Russell Group of universities announced that Art and D&T were no longer to be considered credible prerequisites – not 'challenging' enough for entry into their high-achieving institutions. Politicians of all persuasions reverted to talking about Design as a pre-apprenticeship subject, filed in the box 'vocational' about training rather than education. They seemed to forget William Morris's celebrated observation that training was something you did with dogs. They did sometimes wax nostalgic about a magic moment they had experienced long ago in the craft workshop. It had looked at the turn of this century as though the message about design in schools had been thoroughly received and understood – and yet it clearly had not. The numbers of learners signing up for D&T, and Art and Design, now marginalised in the curriculum, fell off a cliff. Except in the private sector. What went wrong?

Some have argued that Design tried too hard to be all things to all people – raising expectations the discipline could not possibly deliver. That having been confined to woodworking, metalworking and weaving for so many years, it got into the dangerous habit of over-justifying itself: a recipe for disappointment. Others have argued that the very diversity of Design in and across the curriculum led to all sorts of muddles about where the *heart* of the subject lay (process, product or impact), which in turn led to patchy teaching – at first because the Craft generation still dominated in classrooms, later because of the reaction 'when in doubt about simulated design projects, go formulaic' and treat the subject as linear, rigid, constrained. Others still have argued that Design tended to remain physically isolated from the rest of the school, which did not help its supposed integral connections with other core disciplines: this was certainly my experience whenever I was asked to open a shiny new Design wing which conformed to all the latest, increasingly complex health and safety requirements. Out of sight, out of mind? Wearing my Higher Education hat, I also noticed that design graduates – if they went into school-teaching – were much more likely to gravitate towards the art room than the design studio/workshop/space: they did not have the same respect for D&T and its confusing academic claims, coming as they did from a learning environment where 'academic' was still a dirty word.

Whatever the reasons – and they probably include all the above, and more besides – there is no doubt at all that Design in schools has lost ground, esteem and credibility in the early twenty-first century. In political discourse, there has been a strong swing away from Design as a core intellectual/social/academic pursuit: at its most extreme, this swing has taken the form of trying to put the clock back not just to Mr Chippy but to Mr Chips. The big arguments, which used to cut ice, have come to be seen as broken-backed: the claim that designerly thinking is valuable in *all* academic subjects seems to cancel out the more specific and pragmatic claim that design is central to economic/industrial development. Those of us who can remember the excitement, the sense of promise, surrounding design education – in Misha Black's time, the 1970s right through to 1995 – the visionary years, when we all talked animatedly of the experience of design in schools enabling learners to *make a difference* in the cultural world, and about savvy citizens in the modern hi-tech universe – are beginning to wonder whether our conclusions were ever *really* accepted, deep down, by the powers-that-be. I've been around this debate for so long that a student once called me a 'designosaur'. As has often been noted, very few senior people in public life owe their elevated position to design education – even if they do sometimes get misty-eyed about the good old days making table-mats. I once made this point at a design conference in Hanover, and rashly asked the delegates if they could think of a single senior politician who had specialised during their youth in art or design. One hand went up. 'Well, we did try that once, in the 1930s.' I vowed never to use that line in Germany again.

It seems to me the right time to re-group, re-consider, re-research, re-energise the debate, re-iterate, re-present ideas as widely as possible through a variety of media, re-form networks and form new ones, re-consider teaching and learning to design and *through* design, re-explore why design in schools seems such an awkward subject. Time to differentiate very carefully indeed between advocacy and research. Time to make teaching more attractive to those with a design background. Time to have the confidence not to over-claim.

Re-reading MIsha Black's talks and papers, some of what he had to say seems to come from a long, long time ago. The technological context, the economic environment and the political pressures have changed beyond all recognition, although he did predict some of these when first they were emerging. But some of what he had to say remains startlingly relevant, and has strong echoes today: on industrial design and its relationship with engineering on the one hand and art in the other; on the public perception of design; on the importance of making; on premature specialisation in schools and on the best ways to make a career in design appealing to young people, among other themes. Despite nearly half a century's worth of developments within the design profession – from 'Design for Need' in the 1970s to the gold rush of the 1980s and 1990s when many designers lost their bearings; from 'good design' to 'good for business' ; from encouraging producers to encouraging consumers; from 'design' to the more broadly-based concept of 'the creative industries' straddling the old economy and the new – and despite occasional moments of euphoria, these themes remain as important and fresh as ever... perhaps even more so.

"What business have we with art at all – unless we can share it?"

So this 40th birthday volume provides an opportunity to revisit some of Misha Black's key writings, and those of assorted recipients of Medals and Awards, and through them to consider the future of design education – in a variety of contexts – as well as its past and present. Misha Black liked to quote William Morris on access to art and design: "what business have we with art at all – unless we can share it?" Morris also added something – in reply to a question after one of his thunderous lectures – which could almost be the punch-line to this volume. What is the point of design?, he was asked. His reply was "design gives us hope". It has to, by definition.

What a pity Misha Black is no longer around, to update this sentiment...

The International Scene

The Relevance of Industrial Design

Sir Misha Black
Unpublished at the time, written in January 1972

The period of enthusiasm and self-confidence is ended. Few designers now believe that they can change the world by the excellence of their work. Even if they are comforted by the conviction that their activity influences the environment and is thus an aspect of the external forces which affect social development, they know that they are part of political and economic systems which permit execrable social conditions which are tolerated only because they are a fractional improvement on the past.

I have started this paper with these seemingly pessimistic words because they describe the present attitude of mind of many designers and which is more usual than exceptional in the minds of design students. But pessimism destroys the capacity for action. Design without conviction ensures mediocrity. It is possible to be a painter or, conceivably, musician while imbued with unrelieved *weltschmerz*, but it is not possible effectively to design a city or a chair without at least momentary belief in their validity. We must accept our disillusion and the more acute disillusion of the younger designers and yet not allow it to turn into sour pessimism if we are to re-create foundations for the continuation of design and the education of designers into the 1980s. The theories of the Bauhaus are now only partially valid; the sales-oriented creed of the American industrial designers of the 1930s has lost its sales appeal. The civilising influence of Scandinavia is challenged by the extravagant exuberance of Italian designers; Olivetti is suspect and IBM no longer commands uncritical respect. It is significant that at the Assembly of the International Council of Societies of Industrial Design (ICSID) at Barcelona in October last year it was unanimously agreed that it is no longer necessary to include a definition of industrial design in its constitution; what was implied, but not stated, is that the fifty-four societies and councils from thirty-three countries which constitute ICSID cannot agree on what industrial design is. But if the activity cannot be defined, it cannot be practised except as a blind probing towards an instinctively apprehended but shadowy goal. For those engaged in design education this current mood of disillusion and the inability to define goals creates perturbing problems.

Design engineering

The progressive deification of design for machine production from the 1850s onwards is well known to you and I need only remind you of its acclamation in the 1930s when a critic as sensitive as Herbert Read was able to write.[1] 'Whenever the final product of the machine is designed or determined by anyone sensitive to formal values, that product can and does become an abstract work of art in the subtler sense of the term. It is only the general confusion between art and ornament, and the general inability to see the distinction between humanistic and abstract art, and the further difference between rational abstraction and intuitional abstraction, that prevents us regarding many of the existing products of the machine age as works of art, and further prevents us from conceiving the endless possibilities inherent in the machine art'.

[1] Herbert Read, Art and Industry, Faber & Faber Ltd, 1934.

This quotation now reads like memories of a long past youth. More discriminating adulthood sees little art in a typewriter or washing machine, although they clearly have formal and symbolic qualities which, as an adjunct to their mechanical efficiency, can give minor aesthetic pleasure to those who use the commonplace artefacts of our civilisation. A shift of emphasis is important; we no longer look at machine tools and telephones as objects for aesthetic contemplation which are coincidentally efficient machines; we now look at mass-produced objects as technically efficient mechanisms which sometimes have the additional merits of visual and tactile agreeableness. I shall later discuss the problem of objects in which symbolic qualities subsume all other attributes, but in the majority of the products of the light and heavy engineering industries, their appearance is only aesthetically satisfactory if they are the outcome of sensitive formal design which develops from and is dependent on the technical constraints of their manufacture.

This is no place for a dissertation on machine aesthetics as I wish only to make a single point. This is that industrial design, as I understand this ill-defined activity, is an aspect of the totality of engineering design, and success in its practice requires a depth of understanding of the restrictions and potentialities of mechanical and production engineering. Industrial design must, therefore, in the future, be considered as a specialised aspect of mechanical engineering and rooted in its technology as firmly as architecture should spring from the technologies of civil engineering and building construction.

If we isolate industrial design as a discipline, its future in the 1980s must be based on engineering knowledge and experience; the designer must be a special kind of engineer and should not be educated to conceive of himself as primarily an artist bringing qualities of aesthetic judgement and human understanding to bear, from the outside, on problems of engineering invention and design. We do not want to educate engineers with a smattering of human and aesthetic understanding, nor artists with a dilettante knowledge of engineering, but a new kind of engineer able to make the aesthetic judgements, which he must constantly do, with the same authority as that with which he makes mechanical and production decisions.

It may be that by the 1980s the curricula and the attitudes and abilities of academic staff in the engineering faculties of universities and technical institutes may become such as to make largely redundant the teaching of industrial design in colleges of art and design. There are already indications that this will happen, but I still see a need for engineering designers to be educated in the ambiance of art/design/architecture academies to balance the inevitable scientific and technological emphasis at engineering institutions. But this will only remain valid if the art/design institutions are able to provide their students with the essential background of mechanical engineering technology.

The main bulk of industrial design will progressively be undertaken by engineers with a special interest in problems of ergonomics and formal relationships, whether they have initially been educated in art/design colleges or at engineering faculties of universities. I see no future in the 1980s for industrial designers in the heavy engineering industries in particular who are not qualified mechanical engineers. The carving in plaster of machine tools to determine their formal qualities irrespective of mechanical and operational advantage, which has been a popular art/design college exercise, will then be seen only in retrospect as a step towards re-establishing in engineering an awareness of the need for sensitive aesthetic decision. In the light engineering industries the majority of products will attain unassertive formal elegance (which at present distinguishes but a few) by their being designed in their totality by engineers who are aware that style should be an attribute of engineering as it is of literature. But this will still leave large categories of products which require more than elegant engineering to produce socially acceptable results. There are many products in which symbolism is as important as mechanical and operational efficiency. The bodies of automobiles are the exemplar but equally clocks, table-ware, furniture, clothing, television receivers and kitchen equipment appeal primarily to concepts of social pride and pleasure in ownership. This need not be equated only with the artificial standards of a competitive society. The need to obtain pleasure from the possession of things is anchored in the group subconscious and remains as potent today as when Neolithic man first shaped and decorated an earthenware pot.

In these fields of design the need to master the technicalities of production remains essential, but the problems of materials and processes are more easily assimilated as they are based on the ancient crafts of manipulating wood, metal, clay, glass and textiles. The techniques have become more rigorous as artificial raw materials replace the organic and numerically controlled processes take over from the simple machinery of the early twentieth century; but the fact remains that in these fields of design, where the relationship of the artefact to the owner or user is paramount, the capacity of the designer to encapsulate style and thus provide aesthetic satisfaction equals in importance his mastery of the techniques of production. Here design aesthetics subsume utility. The need will remain, therefore, for something similar to the methods of education-through-making which for a hundred years has been the basis of teaching techniques in schools of art and design.

The change during the next decade will be that a designer of glass, china or silver will jettison his pretensions; he will no longer believe, as many do today, that a proven capacity for designing tableware necessarily makes him capable of instructing engineers how to fashion the nose of a diesel locomotive. The fact that craft-based designers can still usefully do so is a criticism of the lack of formal sensitivity of the engineers and is not a justification for a designer's influence expanding beyond the framework of his technical knowledge. The role of the generalised consultant designer with only a modicum of technical experience is a transitory one which will lapse when engineering education achieves its essential maturity. A different role will continue to exist for the generalist designer and this I shall later describe, but let me first consider the role of the craftsman during the next decade.

The handicrafts

From the earliest days of the first industrial revolution there has been an uneasy ambivalence between the roles of the craftsman and the industrial designer. This has been accentuated as man-made materials and automated machine processes have superseded simple machines which initially were only extensions of the craftsmen's hand tools. By the mid-twentieth century it had become impossible for a craftsman to make even a prototype of many mass-produced artefacts without excessive labour – if at all. This is apparent if one considers the problem of making by hand a working model of so comparatively simple an object as a modern fountain pen or a pliable plastic bottle with an ejector nozzle: the craftsman's model bears but little resemblance to the complete impersonality and multiplied perfection of the mass-produced object.

The recognition of essential differences between industrial design, which is concerned primarily with giving instructions to machines, and handicraft, which is a direct expression of the personality and skill of a single craftsman or small group of craftsmen, had led, irrational though it be, to a downgrading of the status of craftsmen. Handicraft was completely excluded from the Hochschule für Gestaltung at Ulm: it is only reluctantly accepted in many other schools of design as little more than therapeutic relief from the more exacting task of designing for industrial production. I believe that this progressive relegation of craft work is misguided. Handicraft, at the height of its achievement, is an aspect of the fine arts – an appraisal of a Sung vase or a Sheraton chair provides sufficient evidence of this fact, but even at the more mundane level of the output of our contemporary craftsmen their work can establish standards of excellence and be a source of self-discovery and aesthetic invention which is denied to the industrial designer seeking an economic solution to an externally imposed problem. It is only to be regretted that the majority of craftsmen throughout the world rarely measure up to their potentialities and now seem content only to make agreeable objects for agreeable people. A period of hand work is, I believe, essential to the development of all designers even if they are destined eventually to work in the more cerebral design disciplines. The subtle differences between a coarse and an elegant junction between two dissimilar surfaces, the problem of the penetration of a three-dimensional form into a larger element, the transmutation of a circular plane into a rectangular plan can only be appreciated by the physical exertion of personally resolving these problems in the malleable materials of wood, metal, clay or in those synthetic materials which can be manipulated by simple hand or machine tools. This making period is essential to all industrial designers, not only to those who will work in the craft-based industries, but equally to those who are being educated as engineers inside or outside colleges of art and design.

An appreciation of the subtleties of formal decision-making is encouraged by the propinquity of those who are content to spend the whole of their working life in the fashioning of malleable materials, and I would therefore wish for the continued co-existence of craftsmen and industrial designers even though their identity of activity is limited as the designer moves rapidly towards a dependence on scientific discovery and technological development as spring-boards for his inventiveness. But if a concern for aesthetic qualities, which an earlier craft experience has inculcated, is lost, then the designer succumbs to a concern only with mechanical practicalities and may produce artefacts which are mechanically effective but socially unacceptable.

From a basis of hand-craftsmanship it is possible to proceed to an understanding of industrial processes which enables the erstwhile craftsman to become an industrial designer. He or she will probably be limited to the design of those products which are small in scale and more dependent on aesthetic decision than advanced engineering technology, but such craft-based industrial designers have produced furniture, textiles, table-ware, radio and television sets, and other relatively simple objects of superb quality.

I know this is an unpopular concept during a period when theories of design methodology are more influential than a concern with aesthetic values, but I believe the path to industrial design from a hand-work basis is a credible one and it has, in fact, been the path by which some of the outstanding designers of today have reached an impressive maturity.

Two approaches to industrial design

I have so far explored two approaches to design. The first is extrovert from engineering technology to the final three-dimensional form of twentieth century objects: the second is introvert from aesthetic concepts based on a craftsman's intuition and instinctive comprehension. I believe both approaches to be valid so long as the practices of the two types of designer are restricted to their capacities: when a craft-based designer applies his aesthetic preconceptions to engineering products such as ships or heavy-duty electrical equipment the result is an aesthetic veneer which easily degenerates into fashionable styling.

If the engineering-based designer attempts to design objects in which symbolic qualities are of paramount importance, then the result is usually pastiche. The two categories of design interrelate and influence each other; stream-lining which emerged from the study of aerodynamics has influenced a whole generation of industrial designers, the craftsman's concern with neat joints and invisible fixings has modified mechanical engineering precepts. But the fact remains that the role of the two classes of design can be differentiated and should be/differentiated in the schools of design. Because most women have some male attributes and most men are partially feminine does not require us to encourage the development of hermaphrodites.

To hell with design

Many students would object to this attempt to classify design into specific, even if interrelated, categories. They transmute the present disillusion of most practising designers into antagonism to the whole concept of the design of objects, the proliferation and the competitive selling of which they interpret as aspects of degenerate society.

I applaud their political and social iconoclasm but question the appropriateness of their professional action. Some of them seek refuge from the enigma of working within a social system which they despise by designing objects of impeccable social value such as medical equipment, or facilities for the disabled; others concern themselves with the design of products which may assist the economic growth of developing countries. I do not question the sincerity of these designed actions, or their value, but they are avenues of escape from the massive centre of our problems, from the reality of our man-made world and the desire of the great majority of people for standards of living and for possessions which comfort them as the warmth of a nest provides security for fledglings.

Men, with the exception of isolated ascetics, desire possessions. It is the duty of designers to reduce their proliferation, so that there is greater value in less. They should cease artificially to magnify the importance of commonplace objects, but people will continue in the 1980s as they do today to desire clothes which ornament as well as protect, houses which provide more emotional satisfaction than an air-conditioned box, possessions which are symbolic of social attitudes. These are fundamental human needs. If the more sensitive young designers will not satisfy them, the unscrupulous second-class designers will fill the vacuum with the tawdry products of their second-class minds.

It has been argued that designers should not attempt to impose their own standards of quality, efficiency, value and beauty on society and that mass popularity is the only ethical criterion. But this specious interpretation of democratic freedom could as easily be applied to architecture and town and country planning and thus continue the despoliation of towns and countryside which has resulted from insufficiently controlled and directed development.

It remains true in urban societies throughout the world that social standards must be imposed by persuasion and legislation once the desire to improve standards is the result of popular agreement. Standards of social hygiene must be enforced, rules are needed to control the siting and height of buildings, pollution must be subject to prohibitive legislation, all children must be required to go to school. Aesthetic standards of design cannot be imposed, even if we knew universal rules of aesthetics, but the designers themselves must be prepared to fight for their own personal standards even if, while doing so, they are conscious of their transience. I am not arguing for a single design attitude. The standards which we believed to be absolute in the 1930s are now disclosed as fugitive, but the need for belief in the designing activity remains; the designer must be convinced of the validity of his approach during the period when he is working. It is immaterial whether he is passionate about classical undecorated forms or has a love for the exuberant elaboration of form and pattern; what matters is that he should believe in what he is doing, whether this continues an established tradition or explores dreams and visions which may illuminate the future.

In general I have thought it necessary to state my belief that the design of objects fulfils a normally justifiable social need if it is monitored by the designer's own sense of personal social responsibility and by his preparedness to demonstrate in this work deeply held aesthetic convictions. I believe also that the capacity to transform conviction into three-dimensional artefacts and systems requires training, knowledge and experience which can result only from years of dedicated study and application.

It would be unnecessary to restate these truisms were it not for the fact that many students and designers are now seeking a general education in art and design at undergraduate level which excludes sustained application to any single technology or group of closely related technologies.

I have dealt elsewhere at some length with what I called the Leonardo syndrome[2], and I return to it only to make clear my belief that there is value in a general approach to art/design education – if the function of those who study in this way is recognised. They will only rarely become designers able to practise as competent professionals (unless they move from generalisation to specialisation at post-graduate level) but they could become business men or manufacturers or civil servants who are imbued with the capacity to make aesthetic judgements, who are able to see the result of their activities in terms not only of balance-sheet figures but also as elements in the man-made world which every generation ennobles or desecrates.

They could, as directors and managers of design, be the men and women who at last halt the flow of physical and visual pollution which threatens to engulf our world.

I see a future, in the 1980s, for courses in colleges of art and design which are considered as an aspect of general education, the 'education through art' for which Herbert Read proselytised throughout his life. They will be the enlightened clients for

[2] Misha Black, 'Design Education in Great Britain'. Nature, No. 5297, Vol. 231, 1 Macmillan

which all practising designers search, able to enter with sensitivity and understanding into the designer/client relationship which determines the success or failure of all design undertakings. Such clients exist-more in Scandinavia than in Britain – but they now do so by exceptional accident rather than by education. I believe such people to be important as accountants, lawyers and doctors and their education needs to be as carefully considered and provided for.

Graphic communication

I have left until last consideration of the function of graphic designers as this is well understood and their education is effectively provided at many schools of art and design. It is unlikely that their activities will change fundamentally during the next few decades: new fields of graphic design activity are already developing which need more flexibility than are provided by the traditional tools of pen, pencil, brush, paper and colour. These fields are in early bloom, but their growth will soon outpace that of the design of books, magazines and advertisement which are still the more common outlets for graphic design. Television graphics require the capacity to visualise movement in addition to two-dimensional relationships, computer typography produces a new technology which must be mastered, audio-visual teaching aids require techniques of communication different from those of the textbooks, museums and exhibitions need to convey ideas and information in addition to displaying objects. Electric signs can be designed to enliven city centres, the naming of buildings and streets can be a minor aspect of environmental design, the complexity of our towns needs maps and signs for direction, complex machinery needs to be explained by word and diagram. The graphic designer can be the communicator between a complex civilisation and its citizens. In the 1980s the graphic designer must move from a dependence on 19th century techniques (and his

" The graphic designer must move from a dependence on 19th century techniques to an appreciation of his social importance."

present defensive attitudes as but a two-dimensional man) to an appreciation of his social importance and the need to master techniques which are appropriate to the second industrial revolution. The need will remain for illustrators of children's books and strip cartoons, but there is a need also for those who can make complexity comprehensive and instruction and direction environmentally acceptable.

Four classes of industrial design

I have identified four categories of industrial design. The first is design for the engineering industries (especially for heavy engineering) which should spring from knowledge and experience of engineering technology. The second is design of objects in which symbolic and human characteristics are paramount, although they may well be manufactured by the engineering industries, which can spring from a craft-based education. The third is design as an aspect of general education to provide potential businessmen, industrial managers and civil servants with the understanding of design processes essential to produce knowledgeable and sensitive clients for the practising designers. The fourth is graphic design, which will become progressively more important as a means of communication during the accelerating second industrial revolution.

I have, however, only explored the fringe of the problem of design in the coming decade. The relationship of industrial design to industrialised building, landscape design in town and country, design for film and television and the use of light, form, sound and electronic control systems to produce scena in which man becomes part of an art-induced liberating ritual – these are all outside the scope of this paper.

But whether the activity be as small-scale as the design of a knife and fork or as large as the concept of a new town, the fundamental creative and technological problems remain. The designers, be they architects, engineers, or those who are responsible for the form of a million plastic pepper pots, are the makers of our environment, they translate into visible form the needs and aspirations of society. They can fulfil these needs at the mundane level of minimum efficiency and maximum economy, or they can transmute them into physical conditions which enrich our existence. As Herbert Read said, in an address to the British Society of Industrial Artists and Designers in 1961: 'The sensibility that coursed along the nerves and veins of countless generations of craftsmen must be made to flow again in the veins and nerves of our industrial designers.' [3] I make no apology for quoting again from Herbert Read, as his understanding of the problems of the industrial designer was profound, but this was because he was not only a man of crystal intellect but also a poet. Poetic sensibility is essential if design is to prosper, if we are not to degenerate into 'perfection without purpose – efficiency for efficiency's sake'. But a poet without a language is silent and a designer without technical knowledge and experience is incapable of making even a minor contribution to humanity.

To design anything, and in doing so perform a minor creative act, requires knowledge and discipline as well as sensitivity. It requires absolute, if momentary dedication to the undertaking. It can achieve maturity only when the technology of the task has been so thoroughly assimilated by the designer for it no longer to be a conscious problem. It is an austere astringent activity which is compensated only occasionally by a momentary sense of achievement.

The painter Pierre Bonnard wrote, just before his death: 'I am just beginning to understand what to paint. A painter should have two lives, one in which to learn and one in which to practise his art.' The problems of the designer are not as acute as those of the painter or poet but at his lesser level of creativity the anguish and the ecstasy remain.

[3] Herbert Read, Design and Tradition. The Design Oration (1961) of the Society of Industrial Artists and Designers. The Vine Press, 1962.

The Designer and Manager Syndrome

Sir Misha Black

Tiffany Lecture given at the Wharton School, University of Pennsylvania, October1973

There is a chasm between talking about merchandising and being responsible for selling, between reading about surgery and actually inserting the scalpel, between being concerned about design and turning a blank sheet of drawing paper into instructions for manufacture. We face problems which did not greatly worry our ancestors. The purpose of business, as the executive once saw it, was purely to make money; the duty of the designer was to produce beautiful objects and environments and, if he lowered his sights to enable industry to increase its profits, he was most certainly, he imagined, prostituting his art. We are wiser, in some ways, than our grandfathers, even if our clearer vision has exposed new problems reaching to the horizon. To the late twentieth-century attitude to business I shall later return, but let me first explain what I believe should now be the concern of the designer.

To be an industrial designer is to be conscious of, and accept, some responsibility for the physical form of our world; to be continuously aware of the shape, size, colour and texture of those parts of our environment which are man-made; or the inter-relationship of component parts, whether they be static or in motion, which produce a single object or a system; and to be prepared to distinguish between those objects and relationships which are aesthetically acceptable and those which fall below our personal standards.

But concern for the condition of our environment and the capacity (or assumed capacity) for aesthetic discrimination do not, in themselves, produce a designer. Concern without the capacity for implementing change is the role of the consumer as critic; to work as an industrial designer technical skills and experience are essential requirements. To be a designer, in the sense that I am now using this generic term, one must not only have the skills but be willing to deploy them to improve the environment and not desecrate it. To this extent design is, or should be, a moral act undertaken within the constraints of the political, economic and social system in which the designer lives and works.

It is a practical art, and as such different from the arts of painting, sculpture, literature and music which can transcend the immediate present and open windows to ecstasy. Design operates at a more mundane level; its concern is with man as a living, mutating, organising and dying entity. It is here that our interests as business executives and mine as a designer coincide. Businessmen are involved in the structure of society, but so is the designer. Businessmen, now desire to improve the physical condition of millions of our fellow human beings and the quality of our lives, and this equates with the ambition or all designers who have escaped despair and enervating pessimism. Business is becoming a profession, design is achieving professional authority. It is now necessary to establish a basis for understanding and co-operation so that business executives can harness design skills to further our common purpose.

I have deliberately used the word 'harness', as the initiative must come from management. A designer without a client is as impotent as an actor declaiming to an empty theatre. The first step in improving design standards is for management to decide that it wishes to do so – from this boardroom decision much good can flow both in financial returns to the company and for society as a whole.

An attitude of mind

I have already suggested that design is an attitude of mind and this must permeate management if more is to be achieved than the purchase of some paintings for the President's dining room and the commissioning of a mural for the staff cafeteria, admirable though such patronage may be. Design is inevitably an aspect of many facets of business organisation. Most business executives are committed to the employment of designers, the only variant being that some are conscious of what they are doing and others somnambulistic. Design exists in the company letter heading, its trade symbol, the livery of its delivery vans, its factory and administration buildings, the furniture and tableware in its staff and executive dining rooms, in the products of its factories and the containers in which they are marketed. It is impossible to be in business without a commitment to design; even a stockbroker has a corporate identity, while those who manufacture products or provide services are dependent on buyers reaction for their very existence.

The techniques for employing and co-operating with architects and graphic designers by forward-looking management are well understood. I regret only that good intention does not more commonly achieve exemplary results, but this is a fault of educational systems throughout the world, in which visual literacy and the culmination of aesthetic discrimination are sacrificed to undue concentration on the development of intellectual faculties. To compensate for their hereditary cataract management should, during this intermediate period, look for wise counsel to support or question their aesthetic predilections. Such counsellors now exist in America and in Britain but they should be selected with the care and attention equal to that which characterises management selection of chartered accountants and lawyers.

The role of the third type of designer which the production industries require is less well understood, so I wish now to describe the function of the industrial designer, who is still too often envisaged as a luxury which can be employed or discarded at the whim of management.

The industrial designer's specialisation is based on anthropometry and ergonomics. It is concerned with the relationship of the users or operators to artefacts or machines whether they be simple domestic or office appliances, complex machine tools, agricultural equipment or control systems. It is the aspect of engineering design that determines whether a hand tool is properly shaped and balanced to ensure maximum efficiency in operation, whether heavy-duty equipment can be operated safely with minimum effort, whether the refinement of kitchen appliances is reasonably related to the capacity of housewives to understand their intricacy, whether the control system of an automobile contributes effectively to safe and enjoyable driving.

The education of industrial designers enables them to participate in the creative processes which are essential to product and system development. This arises partially from the structure of their curricula, which exclude the depth of study in engineering science required of the mechanical engineering undergraduate, and provide time for divergent thinking and developing conceptual attitudes to product and system innovation.

To these is added the advantage of industrial design's being commonly studied in colleges of art and design where the inevitable tension engendered between students of the fine arts and of the useful arts, and the argument and counter-argument by which the artists and the designer attempt to defend their different but related activities heighten self-criticism and set standards of personal achievement and responsibility which I believe to be crucial in developing creativity.

Aesthetics

The second specialisation of the industrial designer is his overt concern with aesthetics, with the formal qualities of objects, with shape, texture and colour, with the visual and tactile relationship of the component parts of machines and products. Separated from mechanism and structure this becomes 'styling' which aims only to encourage sales irrespective of social need; considered as a refinement of the mechanism and structure of industrial products it becomes 'style' which is an attribute of product design and systems of engineering as it is of literature and music.

Style is the signal of civilisation. Historians can date any artefact by its style, be it Egyptian, Grecian, Gothic, Renaissance, Colonial American or Art Nouveau. It is impossible for man to produce objects without, in doing so, reflecting the society of which he is a part and the moment in history when the product concept developed in his mind or was the outcome of the creativity of a group sharing common attitudes and technical capacity. In this sense everything produced by man has 'style', but this can be debased and perverted when factors other than the achievement of excellence become the dominant motivating forces.

The world is littered with products of the engineering industries which disguise their mechanical efficiency (and sometimes inefficiency) with symbolic forms and decorative embellishment, which have only a marginal relationship to engineering necessity and manufacture with the minimum of effort and minimum use of materials and energy. These products are usually the outcome of aesthetic decisions having been made by managers or engineers who are unskilled in doing so. Subjective aesthetic design problems are constantly posed in all design projects which allow for alternative solutions, as do all those which are not conceived at the frontiers of knowledge and mathematically determined.

If there are five such decisions to be made during a design development programme, and if each discloses ten alternative solutions, this can produce 100,000 design variations. If the number of decisions to be made and the possible alternatives increase, the number of possible design variants quickly reaches astronomical figures. The problem is compounded by the fact that some industrial products need consciously to serve symbolic as well as practical needs. This is exemplified by the automobile but is equally apparent in the design of domestic appliances, office machinery and, to a lesser extent, in machine tools and agricultural equipment.

So long as people are not cheated by superficial design into believing that stylish elegance compensates for engineering negligence I see no cause for puritanical objection to dressing-up the ordinary with the glamour of the extraordinary. It differs only in materials and technique from making the visual best of one's personal appearance. The desire to obtain positive aesthetic pleasure and social status from the objects used by man is as old as mankind itself. A concern with the shape and decoration of man-made products is an endemic characteristic of the human race; it stretches from the decoration of Neolithic pots to supporting the structure of nineteenth-century beam engines by classical Grecian columns, from the decoration of Saracen scabbards to the form and livery of the Japanese Tokaido express train. The present need is not to disparage this aspect of style but to ensure that the formal decisions are appropriate to the object, to decide which artefact and systems should be negative and self-effacing and which may proudly and aggressively acclaim the social and symbolic implications of their mechanical purpose. The motor car, high-speed trains and television sets fall into the expressive, symbolic category; machine tools, electronic equipment and hospital equipment have willingly accepted a discrete anonymity in which their formal qualities are the outcome mainly of operational efficiency and economy in production. Some products which are initially expressive recede to a negative acceptance without social overtones and then later burst out again as positive social symbols.

Computers are in the early stages of this aggressive-recessive cycle. They are still a source of pride to their owners but soon to be relegated to commonplace acceptance comparable with the boiler room and the air-conditioning plant, now of interest only to the specialist. The automobile, the most potent symbol of our civilisation, has moved, in 20 years, from brash space-man exuberance to a more subdued and mannerly concern with ground speed images.

The capacity to sense movements in public taste

In a comparative society the need for manufacturers to be aware of the movements in public taste and its effect on sales is an essential factor in marketing strategy. The problem is compounded as attitudes to products and systems now change at accelerating speed.

The capacity to sense movements in public taste does not require clairvoyance. It requires market research (which usually operates negatively by eliminating catastrophically decisions and may sometimes indicate useful lines of technical development) but it also requires a capacity for instinctive comprehension based on a knowledge and understanding of movements in painting and sculpture, an awareness of the attitudes of the most creative and experimental architects and designers and of changing social values. What is happening one year in the studios and experimental workshops will inevitably later influence mass markets; the difficulty is in discriminating between the main stream and eccentric excursions into shallows, and ensuring that the time scale is correct.

The industrial designer, by his association with the fine arts during his education and his continued interest in their influence on public taste, is a useful ally of management and the production team when forward decisions must be made which will influence marketing success or failure. The need to prognosticate social acceptance, to decide whether products have moved from aggressive to recessive positions, is not only an aspect of our capitalist society. It has proved to be a requirement in the Soviet Union, where public reaction to consumer products has also become selective now that the requirements of minimal existence are more easily satisfied. The USSR has established its All Union Research Institute of Industrial Design (VNIITE) to ensure that Soviet manufacturers become aware of the volatile and sometimes seemingly irrational movements in public taste on which the domestic and export sale of industrial products partially depends. The other Eastern European countries are equally conscious of the need to employ the specialised abilities of industrial designers to ensure that their engineering products reflect the style of our century and that their consumer products combine aesthetic satisfaction with efficient utility.

In this field of man/artefact relationships the designers still operate almost entirely subjectively, by hunches which they would find it difficult to describe or justify – except by results. The considerable volume of research work on design method has been concerned with practical problem-solving, and tends to gloss over aesthetic problems as not being a suitable subject for objective analysis. There is a need for more theoretical and case study of the morphology and typology of man-made objects. Until more research work is undertaken we can do little better than follow the advice of Palladio who, in the sixteenth century wrote: 'Although variety and things new may please everyone, yet they ought not to be done contrary to that which reason dictates.'

Reason dictates to management that they should seek specialised skills to augment their own abilities and experience. This can be done by establishing an effective design office within the company organisation, by the engagement of consultant designers or by a combination of both. The latter is normally the most fruitful in large-scale industry. The company design office is in close daily liaison with the other departments with which it must essentially work: with research, product planning, production engineering, sales and publicity. The essential modifications to products which must be made at short notice, the need to watch deviations from the established house style, the opportunity for educational work within the organisation, all fall naturally within the province of the company design office. The consultant makes periodic visits to advise and criticise. He brings to one industry his experience in several, he can talk with the company designer on terms of professional equality, he can talk to management with a freedom not normally enjoyed by employed staff.

But whatever organisational permutation may best meet the needs of a specific industrial or marketing organisation, one irreducible fact remains: the quality of the design programme is absolutely dependent on the capacity of management to appreciate its potentiality. Management is an invisible participant in every design project. The most frequent comment in any design office is: 'It's no use, he will never accept it – you couldn't possibly persuade him to have it', and a brilliant innovation is sadly filed away in favour of a mediocre one which will offend no one, and make a modest contribution instead of a leap forward.

This is not, fortunately, the inevitable rule. There are too many brilliant design innovations in American and British industry to justify despair, but for every innovation which sees the light of manufacture and marketing, a dozen are neglected for lack of the confidence of management in the capacity of their designers, and the lack of confidence of the designers in the vision of their directors or clients.

The essential quality of design is creativity: the capacity for predicting what technology will make possible and what people will desire and need a year or two ahead. As Swift wrote: 'Vision is the art of seeing things invisible,' and the invisible future will be predicted by designers who have been trained to make and then test creative hypotheses. But for designers to work effectively they need the sympathetic understanding of management. I am sure that you, the new breed of managers, will provide the oyster shell in which your designers can be the essential irritant.

Creativity and innovation

Around 1881, when Joseph Wharton established his now world-renowned business school, Queen Victoria wrote: 'Beware of artists, they mix with all classes of society and are therefore most dangerous.' Designers are concerned only with the practical arts, and the danger is thus diminished, but they are, as you are, amongst those who are willing to accept a responsibility for the look and feel of our environment, and if this involves action which disturbs those who wish only to conserve the social and environmental patterns of the past, then Queen Victoria was right and shall continue to be so.

But we are no longer isolated. The council of the Confederation of British Industries has recently accepted a report from one of its committees which reads: 'A company, like a natural person, must be recognised as having functions, duties and moral obligations that go beyond the pursuit of profit and the specific requirements of legislation ... profit alone is not the whole of the matter.' The moral obligation includes a respect for our man-made environment and the elements of which it is comprised. Your generation of business executives and the designers who are your natural allies can ensure that the industries which you will control will improve the physical world and not degrade it.

As Camillo Olivetti said more than 50 years ago: 'A good business is one which *also* makes money.'

I have so far talked about design as though it were a straightforward respectable activity undertaken by men and women who differ only in their technical knowledge and specialisation from the business executives with whom they must collaborate. Viewed from one position, this is an accurate image of the designer's persona. When design is an ordering process changing the inventors' or development engineers' lash-up into a marketable product, or concerning itself with industrial or civic tidiness and good manners, it does not differ greatly from other professional occupation. But this is only one

"For innovation, creative management must be linked with design creativity."

facet of design which has achieved exaggerated importance in our society because only those specifically trained to see are now able to perceive the physical world and suggest how it might be improved. While the world remains sick all who are not motivated solely by greed must combine to construct crutches so that society can continue to exist while it heals itself. Our democratic societies are, however, not monolithic and provide opportunities for new immediate manifestations of the human spirit even if development of the body politic as a whole must be intolerably slow.

There are moments even in the most staid of businesses when a new product or service can be perceived, when a new headquarters building or factory can be planned, when an outmoded corporate image is ripe for complete reassessment. These are moments of excitement which all those involved in the project may share, but they are also the moments when professional competence alone is insufficient. For innovation, creative management must be linked with design creativity, when the visionary capacity of the designers subsumes their daily plain competence. Designers with the capacity for innovation are thin on the ground in all countries, but they do exist and a place should be found for them within the structure of industry and business. Such designers may be uncomfortable companions; they may be motivated by forces which do not answer to the bridle of normal social behaviour; they may well be the odd man out in the necessarily tidy industrial hierarchy, but the odd ball often bounces higher. Design, when it is creative, is not a tidy affair; it is a search for perfection in an imperfect world; but if you, the business executives, will tolerate its non-conformist intolerance, will discover how to harness creativity to your practical needs, then a partnership can be established which will make your working lives more exciting (if less ordered and comfortable) and may make the products and services which you control contribute to a future which will make our present, in retrospect, appear to have been sadly inadequate.

Service, Dignity and Love
A perspective from India

Ashoke Chatterjee
Medallist 1985

"You designers are the link between the substantial shapes and forms of the output of science and technology and the poetry of human sensitivities and needs. That poetry demands that your choices are honest to yourselves and honest to the needs of the country that gave you the opportunity to learn..."
Prof Ravi J Matthai, addressing the first Convocation of the National Institute of Design, Ahmedabad, India.
April 1979

As I write these lines to commemorate Sir Misha's contributions and the 40th Anniversary of the Medal that celebrates his memory, the British Council in New Delhi is concluding a second cycle of discussions with Indian educators on "The Future of Design Education in India". Since The Future is a land none can visit, we can be assured that this issue will continue to engage minds as each generation redefines the purpose of design in changing circumstances. What education may need to sustain it is the purpose of equity which brought contemporary design education to India, and to do this while respecting the world of market forces and bottom-line calculations. There are tensions here that Indian education and educators cannot escape.

Sixty years ago the hope for real change through design education in India was reflected in the seminal *India Report* [1] by Charles and Ray Eames. That little classic was addressed to a newly independent nation seeking transformation from poverty and oppression to a quality of life that could give freedom true meaning. To "wipe every tear from every eye" was the goal Mahatma Gandhi bequeathed to national leadership, an impossible task and yet a context hospitable to a new profession that could take as its inspiration the ethic of "service, dignity and love" recommended by *India Report*. This was the inspiration for the founding of the National Institute of Design (NID), the first experiment of its kind in the developing world. NID was an audacious act, little understood at the time. A country with an unbroken design tradition of millennia had no word in any of its myriad languages to capture the problem-solving process advocated at the Bauhaus and now to be imported into an ancient land pursuing its vision of freedom. 'Design' in those days meant ornamentation, patterns, art, or perhaps engineering and architecture. Market competition, the life-blood of design application, was minimal in a protected market dominated by shortages and a socialist distrust of capitalism. A rigid educational system inherited from colonial times actively discouraged learning by doing, making entry into a design school a calculated risk with little apparent prospect of livelihood. Within this context NID and those who came after it would innovate and establish a new Indian profession that today can attract 20,000 applications for less than 400 seats at one institute alone.

Change has been not merely of degree but of kind. Competition marched through the door with new economic policies of globalisation that have transformed India's markets since the mid-1990s. Technologies undreamt of half a century ago are now in every hand and classroom. Design is recognised as indispensable to survival at home and

[1] *India Report*, National Institute of Design, 1958

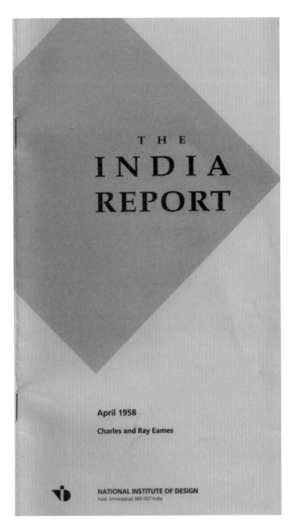

THE

INDIA

REPORT

April 1958

Charles and Ray Eames

NATIONAL INSTITUTE OF DESIGN
Paldi Ahmedabad 380 007 India

Charles and Ray Eames' *India Report*, 1958.

overseas. Fashion is now the dominant image of the profession in young minds, seeking career opportunities globally. Design education like everything else must now be "world class", a term that dominates every discussion of where this society really wants to go. Quality of life can be symbolised by shopping malls, not the spinning wheel which Gandhi made central to an understanding of freedom as self-reliance and caring. 'Service, dignity and love' must now find their way into a market potential estimated by 2030 as a middle class of over 1 billion Indians. While the term designer has transformed from noun to adjective, the basic challenge of 60 years ago is unchanged. Outside glittering urban malls targeted at a market larger than Europe, other Indians struggle for basic food, shelter, clothing and livelihood. Design service is estimated to touch just 2% of a nation of 1.2 billion, perhaps excluding the cellphone revolution. So, has design education broken its promise?

Achievements have been many. Design is now at the top of career aspirations, with attractive salaries and international prospects. From one design college in 1963, there are now over 70, several in collaboration with institutions overseas. Student designers roam the country and continents, while Ivy League scholars arrive to write theses on contemporary Indian design. Role-model professionals have achieved national and global acknowledgement for quality. A decade ago the Government of India announced a National Design Policy for "enhancing the competitiveness of both manufacturing and service industries" with a new motto: "Designed in India, Made for the World". Degree shows on every campus emulate Europe and North America, while an official India Design Council celebrates achievements with coveted awards and the world of fashion lifts designers into the stratosphere of celebrity. According to the British Council report, "Design in India has matured over the years and is booming. By 2020, the potential market for design in India is expected to be GBP 1.43 billion. Only a fifth of the design market is currently tapped". The ability of designers to serve social needs has also been brilliantly demonstrated, even as a 'market' for social design is yet to emerge that can attract young graduates with real-world opportunities sustained by fee-paying clients. The retreat of Government from social responsibilities into privatisation makes this one of the most urgent challenges in making good the commitment 60 years ago to apply design to help lift millions from poverty. Above all is the need for teachers of design willing to commit to the master/apprentice synergy that gave India its early models of excellence. Patient investment in teaching may demand a return to quality over quantity, to real education over the mere transfer of skills. As some brave institutions struggle to sustain that model, tuition shops proliferate their guarantees of slick portfolios and mastery over admission processes.

Not long ago a study by a leading design educator[2] across a sample of stakeholders attempted to understand current complexities. Among his findings were a lack of patience within design professionals, a demand for quick-fixes and that even after 70 years of freedom education in India does not encourage independent thinking, or working with hands and on teams, or openness to interdisciplinary studies over narrow specialisation. Students enter design education thinking in silos. There is a pervasive culture of self-promotion while mindless consumerism takes over. Globalisation is interpreted by dominating models from elsewhere rather than models reflecting local needs. Design learning has become big business, encouraged by a magic wand of privatisation.

"Design schools risk becoming facility centres rather than spaces for value-based exploration."

In this process, design schools risk becoming facility centres rather than spaces for value-based exploration. The early idealism appears to be dwindling. At about the same time as this survey, a group of design professionals came together to offer a contrasting vision of design competencies that India would need for tomorrow. Rather than expand numbers based on old models, they suggested re-imagining design education that could build on what people already know, empowering them to become partners in the shaping of design destinies.

Like so much in India, design is a conundrum of contradictory signals, of hope and achievement as well as of despair as social inequities grow with each milestone of 'progress'. All this came together a few weeks ago on the NID campus celebrating its 38th Convocation. My mind went back to that first graduation event in 1979 at which some 20 young professionals went out into the world clutching a diploma that few outside could comprehend. Now there were over 300 leaving a school that once had been the only one of its kind. NID's Chairperson, a distinguished industrial leader, praised the quality of student achievement while comparing India's present need of over 60,000 qualified designers with 7,000 in the country and 5,000 students in design education. The need was to scale-up and reach the kind of numbers that Asian competitors seem capable of delivering. The Chief Guest was former President of India Pranab Mukherjee. His reminder went back to the beginning, to the need for "inclusive growth for 1.2 billion people" that was "the most complicated challenge humanity has faced. To overcome it,

[2] I.S. Mathur, Design Education in India: Retrospection, Introspection and Perception, NID 2014

all you young designers will have to think differently". Mr Mukherjee called for design that could deliver "sustainable development", a phrase that does not appear in any national design policy document nor in any recent discussion on design education in India. It might well be the actual challenge as well as the opportunity.

At the time of the *India Report* and the founding of a National Institute of Design, the phrase 'sustainable development' was yet to enter consciousness. The concept was implied though not stated then, and again when the UN held its first design conference on the campus of NID in 1979, culminating in the *Ahmedabad Declaration on Industrial Design for Development* [3] which Sir Misha's close colleagues [4] helped draft. The Declaration called on designers in every part of the world to "work to evolve a new value system which dissolves the disastrous divisions between the worlds of waste and want, preserves the identity of peoples and attends the priority areas of need for the vast majority of mankind…" A community of design thinkers meeting in India was anticipating the driving force by which progress across the globe is today understood and measured. The 2030 Vision of the United Nations, endorsed by all its members, comprises 17 development goals for the world community to achieve within the next 12 years. The Sustainable Development Goals (SDGs) [5] recall the vision of a humane society which dominated India's early aspirations "to wipe every tear". Together they suggest a quality of life which design can help achieve, and offer a charter for education. Among the Goals are the eradication of poverty and hunger, reduced inequalities, decent work and economic growth, gender parity, good health and education, clean water and sanitation, climate action, and the creation of livable cities and communities. In design terms, one goal stands out: 'Responsible consumption and production' (Goal 12). Together, the SDGs breathe new life into that early hope of design as an ethic of "service, dignity and love", and into that call from Ahmedabad for a new value system to reduce waste and want. Science, technology, poetry and integrity come together here to express a quality of life that is about caring for each other and for the earth that is our shelter. In 2018 that quality can be the hope of design education that is in India and for India.

[3] UNIDO-ICSID-India 79: Design for Development. Ahmedabad Declaration. NID

[4] Among them were John and Sylvia Reid, Victor Papanek, Herbert Ohl, Carl Aubock, Gui Bonsieppe, Shoji Ekuan, Arthur Goldreich, Alexander Neumeister, Basilo Uribe, Yuri Soloviev and H Kumar Vyas.

[5] 2030 Agenda. Sustainable Development Goals: Division for Sustainable Development, UN-DESA. New York, 2015

Focus on the Human Being
A perspective from Latin America

Professor Santiago Aránguiz Sánchez
Medallist 2013

During advances in science and technology, changes in the paradigm of education –
and in the middle of a complex panorama of the development of humanity – there arises
the adventure of dreaming of a better education, not only for design, a better education
where people are the centre of all action to achieve a more just and balanced society.
The complexity of modern life and the accumulated fatigue of a consumer society, plus
immense imbalance where poverty, human rights, freedoms and opportunities to purify
democracies appear as priority demands to envisage a better horizon.

From the perspective of the Southern Hemisphere, Latin America is struggling with the
unknowns of very different countries where the training of professional designers shows
projects with very high percentages of interest in new technologies and programs that
ensure student undertakings and an early access to the market that allows them to
recover the onerous investments of the cost of their studies.

From the theory of design we can imagine that the challenges of our professional activity
must change the essence of our objectives, putting the human being as the main factor
in our activity without neglecting the equilibria with the prevailing economic model. Today
we see clearly how interest in the values of culture has declined – the depredation of
nature, insensitivity to the cultural and natural heritage and the values of indigenous
peoples.

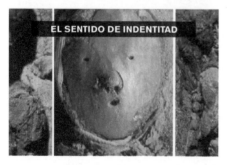

Images from Professor Sánchez' Medallist address at the RCA, 2013.

Design must be political in that it must raise its voice from within its frankly humanist gaze – and for that it must understand the social sciences, it must base its projects together with the other actors in the political field and it must not be a subject that is integrated at the end of processes where its voice is already condemned to silence and acceptance of decisions.

From a real perspective of countries that do not contribute mainly to the gross product of the world economy – and whose economies are based on exporting raw materials without added value – challenges of great interest to the discipline arise. However, a greater effort should be made to work on issues of creativity, as contributions to the knowledge of our identities. The countries of Latin America are rich in raw materials, but their greatest wealth is their people, their natural scenery, their scenic beauty, their poetry, their music and cultural expressions born of their material and immaterial advantages. That wealth must be known and interpreted to be shared with the world in healthy coexistence rather than with accelerated competition.

Thousands of studies are carried out in our Universities to encourage design as an activity that is fully justified in the field of higher education, and this involves many of them on a focus on market studies, economics and business, new and very advanced technologies and openings to businesses that, in the view of ambitious students, meet the expectations of rapid or short-term success. Along the way, the subjects that made design an openly humanistic activity have been lost.

The history of art, ethics, cultural anthropology, aesthetics, sociology, psychology, and drawing are in a clear retreat from the curriculum. The view of society and the future has changed, the centre is no longer the social perspective at whose heart is the human being. Certainly, the objectives are focused on business and economic growth, rather than the personal fulfilment. However, it is understandable if the demands of state policies do not orient the direction of education and its culture.

What we really see is a persuasive disorientation and the absence of a long-term future dream, leaving us with a "country reality" that zigzags every four years in its plans. Teaching, research, outreach and connection with the environment are the structure of university education; this formula has a basic logic because everything leads towards the creation of knowledge for the benefit of society whose objective is people, family, environment, way of life and future, clearly a humanist way of thinking ...

The reality is that somewhere the process has become distorted, so much so that there must be a regulatory body to ensure compliance with these objectives. Viewed from the point of view of design as a discipline, the need arises to create a policy that orders participation as an essential activity in the labour market and equal participation in government projects where designers are properly incorporated into the projects of all kinds emanating from the different ministries that constitute the state. That achievement would begin to imagine the future of education in design.

The "country reality" is something else, in this and in any country on the planet. Topics such as sustainability, the environment, natural resources, wealth to know and known wealth, poverty, health, culture and education, natural disasters, communications and entertainment, among many other topics, fill pages of news in the media. Design can and has done much to collaborate, participate and change the state of things. The nine semesters of a university student should be a time of great change for a professional of the future, they are in the ideal space to share and to know reality, the university as the centre of interactions and interdisciplinary activities – not as a centre for producing professionals in the "country reality".

I imagine the designer of the future as a sensitive being and great connoisseur of the impressive impact that understanding his own senses will have, a designer who is clearly aware of the importance of the method of observation beyond the eye. To master the concepts of seeing, watching, observing, contemplating or even being ecstatic with his vision. How can the external world be interpreted if the universe that inhabits us is unknown? Hearing, taste, touch, smell and other senses are powerful tools with which to create and communicate to others ... I want to think about a design career where imagination has no limits and where emotions occupy a privileged place in the design of experiences or solutions for people. A career that delivers ways of understanding society, and its evolution. This is not just restricted to designers of the future; every professional must have access to this culture. Obviously, the knowledge, science, technology and the changes that the earth undergoes develop rapidly and it is not possible to stay still or remain in underdevelopment, especially in countries like ours that have not yet overcome such basic problems as housing, health and education.

Every University project bases its objectives on the real world and with legitimate aspirations that make possible changes in the short, medium and long term. The bureaucracy and those who do not know our discipline, demand methodologies, indicators and systems that can be perfectly controlled to guarantee the success of the programs. Teachers spend a lot of time in complying with the indicators to the detriment of their own vocation to encourage creation as a principle at the base of all things. This fictitious structure removes the marrow from the training of the new designers but it complies with what is determined in the model that governs our organisation.

The future of education will have many variables that will continue to be shared according to the trends of prevailing models; my wish is that they focus on the human being to collaborate in the solution of their problems of identity, their fundamental values, that open spaces for growth and coexistence.

The challenges of design are the challenges of all disciplines, the challenges of the future will help us to reflect the world of artefacts where so many thousands of designers have focused their work can change and compel us to see the future with different eyes: putting your eyes on the nature and beauty of your contemplation, while the world of objects designed and manufactured by man distracts us, nature leads us to the essentials...

The Future with China

Reflecting the world in which we live

Professor Catherine McDermott

Award 2016

The best design educators inspire students not only to imagine their own, but a shared future. So if the future confirms China as a leading creative hub, is the UK design education sector investing enough in this changing world?

A more developed relationship with China's design education makes sense to support UK industry in the context of the new post-Brexit economy. And a review of thinking on China, too often seen in terms of fee income, is overdue. So is our confidence that UK design education is implicitly 'more developed'. Of course British design education has much to take pride in. In the 19th century we were the first country to teach industrial design practice and we still lead in innovative design education. The danger however is always in a failure to understand the competition and UK design education now needs to interrogate important questions. How are design educators future-proofing a more competitive era in contemporary Chinese design? Are we moving on from the millennium catchphrase 'Made in China, not designed in China' and as a sector, understanding the opportunities the Chinese creative industries can offer the future UK?

The UK Government invests in teaching Chinese language and culture across all education, expanding funding to deliver Mandarin programmes, cultural exchange and industry internships. The statistical challenge however is that these exchanges are skewed towards the Chinese learning English and studying in the UK and not vice versa. While the Higher Education Statistics Agency documents increasing numbers of Chinese students studying fashion and design in the UK, the numbers of home students studying and experiencing design in China remains low. If this exchange imbalance continues it could challenge the future success of UK design education and UK-trained designers.

In 2018, what does the relationship between design education in the UK and China look like? We know that since the millennium China has rapidly expanded its home design education capacity and continues to favour international training in terms of the academic and design job markets. Anecdotally we know that Chinese design education has a major lack of design PhDs, which foreign universities can help fill. China continues to place a strong value on UK design education with Britain remaining a favoured destination for both design education (with fashion, for example, seeing a steep rise in applications) and the development of shared curriculum development and delivery.

But the wider picture remains a concern. Consider the evidence from the Creative Industries Federation that the UK, and by implication design education, is not doing enough to tackle the shamefully low number of BMEs working in the sector, while clearly they should be, diversity and inclusion are not top agenda items for design education. Think about the unconscious bias in the way UK design curricula favour Western design. Why are Chinese designers at the height of their careers, like Huang Chunmao, Song Tao and Ma Cong, so little known in the UK? And why are leading UK design schools not only failing to include 21st century China across their curriculum, but so slow in appointing ethnic Chinese staff to Professorial positions and Honorary Awards? UK design education might consider the two words the actor Frances Dormand used to close her 2018 Oscar acceptance: inclusion rider, a clause that stipulates all work should reflect the world in which we live.

This prejudice (or at best short-sighted thinking) in UK design education comes into play at different levels. As educators, how do we judge the 'subtle' pressure on Chinese design students to take Western names? Could it be because we don't learn the pronunciation of Chinese given names? These tensions are not all our own 'fault'. Even for native speakers Mandarin is an extremely difficult language to learn. There are real, and very serious, fault lines, not least the freedom of expression central to our understanding of creative practice. Neither does China always make things easy for 'the West' with transparency of decision making; it is layered, complex and hard to understand.

Take the example of the 2018 Bloomsbury Gallery exhibition, showcasing work from leading Chinese design tutors now in their 40s, including Beijing-based Huang Chunmao's tableware for the Hanghzou G20 Summit, Shanghai textile designer Song Tao and Nanking's Ma Cong. The show becomes much more important when you understand its provenance from the International Exhibition Agency, China's largest cultural events group. The CIEA is more or less equivalent to China's British Council, overseeing how China's visual culture is presented to the world including the Venice Biennale. It is very different from the collaborative approach of the British Council with whom I have been working on competitively funded projects for over a decade.

The British Council's mission is to build the international brand of UK education through collaboration across countries. In partnership with the British Council, my educational projects in China have included Dream Lab – a five-year, £1.5 million design science competition to showcase UK design education's interdisciplinary expertise.

Porcelain designed by Huang Chunmao for the G20 Summit, 2016.

Credit: Talking Through Internships 2018

The deliverables included three online competition briefs for 400 Chinese teams in 150 Chinese universities and UK students and researchers. In the UK the impact on design education came from direct contact with the Chinese teams via a specially designed online platform giving UK tutors an understanding of Chinese teaching practice and internationalising the curriculum across two countries. In 2014, this was extended to electronic engineering, with additional briefs to address concerns of falling recruitment in engineering and the low career take up by women in both countries. Creative Challenge (2014) included staff from six universities, combining electronic engineering (Universities of Coventry, Central Lancashire and Huddersfield) and design (Universities of Kingston, Sheffield Hallam and the RCA). It was a steep learning curve – not least because the differences in student responses across both countries were nowhere near as marked as we anticipated. We saw the potential of a Sino-UK design network to create new ways of working across different design education systems.

My current design education project *Talking Through Internships* also tackles a problem identified by the Chinese and UK Governments: there are not enough designers connecting practice across the leading creative hubs of Shanghai and London. Our pilot is pioneering change through student designers from the Design Schools of Kingston and Jiao Tong universities experiencing a month's internship in design companies in Shanghai and London respectively.

Instead of spending time in the universities, the students go straight into major design companies like the advertising agency BBH London + Shanghai, Priestmangoode, Seymour Powell, Tangerine and Crystal Shanghai. It has not always been easy or smooth, but all the students reported transformation in their appreciation of their host country's designers and design processes. In turn, the host companies in both countries have experienced fresh eyes and thinking from would-be design practitioners schooled in different educational processes, adding value to existing projects and to company staff's understanding.

Building partnerships across design education in China and the UK can only help to build success, increase opportunities and support a more resilient and safer future.

Against Logical Systems
A perspective from Italy

Ettore Sottsass Hon RDI
Medallist 1999

I am very honoured and pleased to receive this award and also, in a way, to be able to take part in our unfaded memory of Misha Black – who was such an interesting and important figure in the history of contemporary, and particularly British design. I also wish to thank all those people who for this honour thought of my name, thus letting me know that there are people in the world who appreciate what I have thought and done during the many, many days of my life.

There is the problem of the title attached to the medal, though as a matter of fact this is not really a problem, but an excuse to talk... otherwise what is there to talk about? The title of the medal is "Services to design education". The question, perhaps, arises from the fact that I have never, never actually *taught* at any school. I have occasionally shown my works to students and talked to them about the adventures of my working life. In recent years I haven't even given lectures any more. I ask audiences for questions and do my best to come up with answers, by telling various stories and describing emotions; by gossiping a bit and sometimes mentioning thoughts that come into my head; not systems of thought, but nomadic observations, *fragments* of thought. I don't think I have ever really been capable of developing a global, linear and continuous system of thought that might work for myself, let alone anybody else.

When I was a young man going to the university of architecture, I didn't attend lectures in the afternoon. The reason was that I was too busy visiting an anarchic painter friend of mine. At the time this man seemed old to me, but he knew a lot about contemporary painting. My painter friend had lived in Vienna, and in Munich in the "Blaue Reiter" days; and he had even lived in Paris... I was eager to learn. At home I did watercolours on my own, and used to take them over to get his opinion. My painter-sage friend used to say nothing. He would talk about other things but then, bit by bit he would tell me stories which, if I was alert enough, should have made me realise what was wrong with my watercolours. He didn't offer me notions. He offered me thoughts.

Only once, when I had squeezed a lemon yellow straight out of the tube, my painter-friend said to me: "Look, Sottsass, you can't use a yellow like that". And I said: "But I saw it in a painting by Matisse", and he simply replied: "When Matisse painted that yellow he was fifty. You, Sottsass, are eighteen". What my painter friend was giving me was not a "notion". He was encouraging me to think about all the things that come before and behind the notion. He was encouraging me to tread by myself on complicated ground, on ground that wasn't clear, on the unknown grounds of existence; he was encouraging me to ask myself questions, to train myself to think... he was encouraging me not to be content with what was written on that tube of paint. "Lemon yellow" is not enough... My old friend was really also educating me to think that "a thousand pieces of information do not yet make a thought"; which could also be taken to mean "a thousand treatises on engineering do not make a work of architecture", or even that "a thousand treatises on 'design management' don't bring a single design into existence." With all this, my old anarchic friend was also suggesting that I ought not to put too much trust in global, linear and continuous systems...

Then, with this first subtle suspicion, day after day, existence itself, the events of my own existence and the actual landscape of planetary existence, educated me to think that the whole history of human tribes is nothing but a constant piling-up of fragments; and that it is at the same time a continuous, agitated effort to justify by a global logical system, by some sort of global acceptance, by some form of global distraction, the presence of the dark and ominous Himalaya of fragments, the presence of incessant unanswered questions, the incessant presence of dark uncertain, unknown places.

In the many millennia of history, someone has always been trying to discover some sort of logical system, some kind of binder to hold the abandoned fragments together: the logic of magic, the logic of yoga, the logic of sex; of silence, of solitude, of religion, of the mind, of numbers, of science, of chance, of chaos... At the end of the second millennium (another virtual sign), as far as I can tell from what I have seen, heard and even tried out on myself during my existence, I think it can be calmly stated that every system of thought which attempts to be global, which attempts to glue together all the fragments that are scattered about in places and in time or even scattered throughout the universe among the stars and innumerable galaxies, every system of human thought can answer nothing except the brief, very brief, almost ridiculous questions about the more or less complicated everyday practicalities that occupy so much space – or no space at all – within the permanent, asphyxiating, indelible question.

I too, when dealing with everyday practicalities, have a logical system. Partly mine and partly invented by others, it sticks together brief moments of my existence which are more epiphanies than realities. It is the system that allows me to tie together more or less pleasant automatisms, in a sequence of more or less convinced virtual decisions: the sound of the alarm going off and my eyes opening, and eyes opening with my hand turning the bathroom tap and then my hand picking up the toothbrush and squeezing the toothpaste tube, followed by other gestures and gestures and gestures and gestures. I am capable of linking my teeth and the toothpaste and toothbrush, again due to my trust, to my total by now automatic trust in some sort of logical system, even with that very strange breech in the wall of the house that is the front door through which I go out; and with that front door I can link the street – Via Dei Fiori Oscuri (Dark Flowers Road) – that I have to walk along to get to the office... and innumerable other automatic gestures. But the globality of my personal system is very brief; I don't go beyond a few districts of the city. I know very few systems that attempt to explain the city, and they are certainly not global. Actually, I don't know any at all. At this point I suppose I ought perhaps to be more precise. But then I also think that maybe it's better never to be too precise. I think precision can only be applied when we're talking about the toothpaste tube and the toothbrush. But I don't think we can take precision much farther than that. In any case the comedy continues.

Industrial culture also claims to possess global, logical systems. Contemporary industrial culture likes to call its global systems "progress" or "prosperity", or sometimes even "civilisation" (terms that haven't been invented long and have never been clearly defined). With these high-sounding titles, systems of global logic of contemporary industrial culture spread all over the place, to reassure the planet that the solution has (or nearly has) been reached, to invite planetary tribes not to waste time thinking, because everything has already been very carefully thought out and carefully foreseen, to punish other proposals as obstacles in the quick, straight and certainly victorious path of the great global theory.

The winning global logical theory lays down conditions that are necessary, indeed indispensable, to its continuity and renewal and destiny. So deep is the fear that the whole vision designed by global logic may collapse that, with the passing of time, the conditions set for survival grow heavier. They comply with increasingly narrow, more closely defined, more scientific processes – as people like so much to call and to practise them nowadays. The conditions, the instruction booklet, the little red book, are increasingly part of a general, global theory and practice.

In contemporary industrial culture the prime condition is: to accept, back and promote any kind of competitive attitude, by accepting, backing and promoting scientific techniques of street-war aggressiveness, of a guerrilla warfare in which no holds are barred and no rules exist, where not even the medieval rules of chivalry exist, let alone the least sign of ethical awareness. A further condition is to accept, develop and spread more or less scientific techniques of persuasion – a new way of saying seduction or plagiarism even, meaning to convince at any cost by the use of violence, by the use of deviant, pointless and false arguments. I cannot go round Milan without being accosted by some half-naked lady photographed on the walls shouting at me to buy Armani underpants or Scotch whiskey, or lured by a sea with palm-trees and another half-naked young lady prancing about on the beach and flashing all her teeth to tell me, even if I don't know her telephone number, that I must go and see her ...all stuck onto Milan's very long and noisy trams...

"This is information", they say. "It's advertising", they say. "It all depends on the creativity of the advertising agencies". They say: "He's a genius at creativity! He used Schiffer's face to make her eat a cat fattened on a special petfood." "He's a creative genius", they say: "This is advertising". In the marvellous theory for the global, unfailing elimination of human unhappiness, there is a further condition, namely: to accept the rigorously rational – positively scientific – study of sales techniques, mixed with the rigorously rational, or rather, scientific, study of "what can be sold?" This is a subject normally turned into the primitive and idiotic question: "What do people like?" and into other painfully fundamental questions like "How much does it cost?" or "Is it cost-competitive?" or "How is it marketed?" In mass industrial culture the answers to these questions naturally have to have a scientific substance; the answers have to have the blessing of scientific method...

One of the last conditions required by mass global culture is "design", or rather, "industrial design": because design (as far as the meaning of the word design is concerned) has always existed in the history of humankind. It existed even before the invention of writing; it has been there ever since somebody started drawing lines or dots on bits of bone – heaven knows why – maybe because that person wanted to know more about existence? Design has existed ever since somebody decided to paint the skulls of his or her dead with an ochre colour – who knows why – maybe because that person wanted to know more about death? Nobody knows and nobody ever will, but could it be surmised perhaps that with those dots and lines the history of design had begun?... Industrial design on the other hand is, at the most, two hundred years old and we may also wonder: "Why does industrial design exist anyway?"

The question of why industrial design has existed in the two hundred years of its history, which has followed the history of industry, has been given various and diverse answers in different countries. Britain and Europe had an industrial design based on the idea that beautiful things would help to make people nicer and better, and it was also believed that

48

'Valentine' portable typewriter designed by Ettore Sottsass for Olivetti in 1968. He described it as "a machine designed to keep poets company on lonely weekends in the country".

industrial culture would have assumed the ethical responsibility for making people nicer and better, through the conquest of an expected prosperity.

In the United States, industrial design has always been thought of as a service, not to people but to industry itself. The idea is that if products have sex appeal as a result of their design, more of them would be sold. So industry would get bigger and send out more products with sex appeal. Then it would get even bigger, and the designing of that sex appeal would be decided by the marketing-scientists, and the designers would have to listen to the marketing-scientist, and so on. Or rather: "So be it". Everybody knows these stories and I have repeated them here rather hurriedly, maybe with a touch of anxiety.

I personally am very glad that industry exists and I am also very glad that designers exist for industry. I am again glad, very glad indeed, that prosperity does exist here and there on the planet. I would be more pleased, much more pleased, if so-called prosperity existed everywhere, and I would again be very, very, very much more pleased if in those parts of the planet where prosperity does exist, I mean where this special state of things exists, it could be accompanied – who knows, maybe with the aid of design – by thoughts about existence and not just thoughts about prosperity; and I mean thoughts about the relationship between people and what they can or cannot do, with what they do or do not produce for themselves and for others; thoughts which everybody ought also to have about this poor powerful bright and bitter planet flayed by our human presence on it; thoughts about the relationships which everybody has with other people, the relationship which each one of us has with the passing of our mortal time, the silent invasion of nostalgia, the unknown and the uncertain. So you see, these are thoughts from which science, industry and prosperity can distract us but from which neither science nor industry nor prosperity can ever relieve us.

It could be that everything I have been telling you about and which people would like to happen, is really only a facile utopia. I really don't know if it will happen, or rather, I know very well it won't, but this doesn't stop me proposing it...

" I could say that the future does not exist, because when the future is there it has already become the present."

I don't think a lot about the future. I could say that the future does not exist, because when the future is there it has already become the present. Perhaps there are projects for the future but when projects for the future are vast, when they claim to propose futuristic global solutions, then I don't trust them too much, indeed I don't trust them at all. I am reminded at once that all the contemporary, aggressive agitation about the future is ultimately just a melancholy way of ignoring all the failures, all the fears, all the disasters and all the violence that the present brings with it and by which the present is designed.

What can be seen of the future on the horizon doesn't look very clear or promising. It promises the Internet, it promises mergers between powerful banks, it promises package tours and Club Méditerranées around the world; it promises AIDS and faster aircraft; it promises cloned sheep and goats, and children via solitary frozen masturbation and pornography; it promises ever more efficient man-maiming mines, ever more rapid gunfire and flatter television sets; with space increasingly cluttered with flying fragments of machines, increasingly filled with well-controlled and well-managed news. It promises everlasting happiness.

I know a few young people whom I admire a lot. They too, like me, live in perplexity but they are also tough. I hope they will carry on thinking and thinking and thinking; thinking thoughts that encapsulate the idea of cooperation, patience and compassion, that contain curiosity, doubts and uncertainties and a challenging calmness. I hope that these special young people will never stop thinking, not only about "practicalities", but also about destinies that are carelessly excited and accelerated by all that is secret, obscure, unknown and dangerous behind these daily practicalities which are called "the necessary reality".

Let It Be

A perspective from Mexico

Professor Gonzalo Tassier
Medallist 2008

I receive this award on behalf of every one of the Mexican designers dedicated to the noble task of teaching design in my home country and on behalf of all of those who have taught me to teach design.

I would also like to thank all those who made this award possible. Those who promoted my nomination, those who offered their testimonies and to all my students with whom I have had the pleasure to discover teaching.

Before today, in Mexico, we knew little about the existence of this very important award on the design teaching field, much less we were aware that Sir Misha Black's Award would travel to a Latin American country.

Professional Graphic design is very young in Mexico, our schools were founded only ten years before Sir William Coldstream would receive the first medal, thirty years on, here we are... but hey! Better late than never.

I am aware of the responsibility I am taking on; it is the least you can expect after receiving this award.

I spent more than ten years tutoring Graphic Design at the Universidad Iberoamericana on an advanced semester because I realised that the student's first steps were exasperating. If the comparison is allowed, I enjoy much more teaching how to ride a bicycle than pushing the pram... maybe, teaching design is more similar to holding up the bicycle while the rider learns to maintain the balance.

My formulas have been always empirical, unorthodox, many times I was accused of being a too tolerant teacher, liberal, generous... an extremely laid back teacher, after more than thirty years I still think that it is easier to reach the port if any storm is avoided, the students should navigate without somersaults. I find it hard to speak about myself, on how I came to teach, but today putting modesty aside, I will make an exception. I got to this point thanks to a gift: the gift of drawing, of seeing, of transforming, of giving things back to paper in another form.

Drawing is something that amuses me, it makes me smile. I like to design from the premise: "and why not?" I like to give image a chance, because images can manifest under many shapes. I like to engage in deep analysis, I like to steal the objects' soul and only then draw them.

We have heard repeatedly that there's no design without an idea, but no one actually can explain where the ideas come from! And no one seems able to pinpoint where design comes from either.

I think that drawing has a grammatical structure, it can be conjugated, it has rhythm, metrics, poetry and follows a set of rules, but once you know them, you can break them pursuing the new in a quest for creation. We are here to celebrate teaching, the academy, the school in its original sense, maybe as Plato understood it, although I conceive it as much more amusing, maybe because our field of work, design, is fun and bursting with colour by definition.

Today I intend to share 'My Philosophy on Teaching Design', but I am afraid this will prove disappointing as there is no such philosophy, I am just a romantic who strongly believes that a well-looked-after romance gives the best fruits and if it is properly cultivated will last a lifetime.

I want to thank and acknowledge the various teachers that at some point noticed me and believed that I could teach, simple as that, just teach. Specially Jesus Maria Cortina, who recently passed away. Professor Cortina thought I could teach advertising design to communicators and opened up a subject called "Production of Originals for Printed Materials", some weeks on, the students re- named it "Creative Advertising" and later on I re-named it again as "Group Therapy".

It was there that we conceived one of the methods that transform the pain of looking for an idea into the happiness of finding one, without neglecting the stage of self-thinking and the solitude of creation. This method is still in usage in my studio: we get together, we discuss, we share, we go up and down, we change direction, and finally we decide and solve. Pretty much as I decided to change faculty and leave for a design school, where I finally realised that design can't be taught, but it is rather discovered little by little, from a dot to a line, outlining and marking an entire life.

At the University, the curricula included strict exercises from the Ulm school: grids, rhythms, thickness, etc and all that discipline that I ignored, so I started to introduce elements of freedom in communication such as humour, imagination and old techniques such as chalk, gouache, finger painting, scissors and everything that would help my students lose their inhibitions.

We started to introduce reality to the study plan, my student's projects needed to be real, have an actual client, I didn't care if it was their auntie's corner shop, their dad's business or even design a sticker for the bumper of their cars.

  A real project
  A real country
  A real need
  A real problem to solve

If they couldn't find an actual project, they should contribute designing something for the university: posters, leaflets, fanzines, etc.

For me designing is a continual unrest, a non-stop question... Would Beethoven ask himself which movement goes next?... the movements are built note by note on a rigid pentagram of discipline, following tempos, using each one of our five senses, not only with hearing in music, and not only with sight in design. Possibilities are endless, maybe that's why they are called "possibilities", and if it is possible it can be done.

I recall the sentence: *"If your project is possible, we deliver in an hour, the impossible takes longer..."*

With this, I just want to say that I have spent fifty years in unsettled movement, in constant anguish, looking how to transform a line, a figure, how to put a new colour next to another, a stroke that transmits movement, a sudden discovery that makes you smile. Drawing follows grammar, from there comes the new wave of 'image semantics'.

These days, a student who buys a computer, carries around more design inside that little box than the design I have gotten inside me for over sixty eight years. The thing is that another million designers bought the same computer, an identical electronic machine that knows how to do things at the click of a button, so it is up to that man behind the keyboard to be a better human being, a wiser man, a more beautiful, a more compassionate one, more sympathetic with their fellow men, he should wear down the insensitivity barrier, in other words, unblock the pores and learn to feel, rejoicing over the fact of feeling and share those feelings, that's the school's duty.

And here is where the teacher comes in.

The teacher must be no more than a loving guide, a motivator, a confidant, a quiet smile.... When students arrive in college they have been scolded too many times, the least that they need is more intimidation.

One of my favourite quotes is a short one: "Amaze me!"

For forty years I have been a loyal reader of *Graphis* magazine; whatever is inside always amazes me. Many times the results have pleasantly surprised me and in many others they have surpassed my expectations.

There is an scenario that frightens me and it is when I come across an unusual proposal from one of my students, a proposal that I might or might not accept, that I might or might not criticise, luckily there is room to say "let's give it a go, why not"... in general the results are positive. Something that was very convenient was the creation of a marking tribunal; this would absolve me of any injustice. The day of the exam the works would be exhibited for everyone to see.

In silence the students would compare their own work with the rest until they came up with a mark. Then the group would decide on a new mark for each one of their fellow students, and finally I will add up mine. This tripartite method would give a fair and balanced grade, away from academic subjectivity.

And this was pretty much how my life was at the University... Mondays, Wednesdays and Fridays, from seven to eleven for many years, until a series of trips connected to my studio practice obliged me to quit.

Back then, Manuel Alvarez was the Director of the Design Department, his name Is relevant because he studied his Masters degree here at the Royal College of Art under Sir Misha Black's tutoring. Before coming here, I told him I was going to be at his school and he told me that Sir Misha Black was a short man, who wore a black hat, smoked more than myself and was very strict in judging projects.

Manuel had to present his final project, a petrol station serving fuel by gravity, without pumps, and Sir Misha Black was a judge of the project, so Manuel went to his office, without his knowledge, measured his height in the mirror where he used to comb his hair and that was the height he used to present his work... At the end of the presentation Sir Misha Black secretly thanked him for the attention to detail because projects were always presented for taller persons.

Manuel requested a work program and here is the proposal I wrote at the time that resembles my philosophy for teaching design.

> Dear Manuel, in response to your kind request for a "detailed" study plan for the Design assignment for the final semesters... I have a simple reason for the delay: I have tried three or four times to start writing but it has been fruitless... I just don't know where to start.

Today it is different, I'm determined to pull a string off the hank and at least draft some ideas that justify my presence here:

If my students understand the aesthetic pleasure that for me is the image of going back home on a bicycle with an "English cap"... after nearly finishing a day of work... I will feel satisfied:

> If I get them to understand that art is love,
>
> If I get them to trust in themselves and in what they have to express,
>
> If I get them to be apostles,
>
> If I get their works to be the fruit of a deep rebelliousness against what surrounds them,
>
> If I get them to distinguish what is worthwhile from what is worthless,
>
> If I get them to – like in the nursery – follow their own creativity, their autonomous creativity without boundaries,
>
> If I get them to follow their impulses,
>
> If I get their tears to be fertile,
>
> If I get them to know how to see and grow full of stimuli to feed their soul,
>
> If I get them to exile stupidity from their lives, the stupidity that translates into inconsistency and massification,
>
> If I get them to understand their small problems that today seem insoluble,
>
> If I get them to read, understanding what they are reading and understanding who wrote it,
>
> If I get them to commit to their own truth... to open their eyes to the world of graphics, of paintings, of what can be seen... I will be satisfied.

We learnt from you the catchy phrase that says "Let It Be", and that is pretty much the same philosophy applied to all my students, I let them be.

Design Education

Personal Failure

Sir Misha Black
Written January 1971, published in Ark issue 48

When I was a boy at school the only thing I was good at was ART. This consisted of designing wallpaper patterns which were bowdlerised versions of William Morris reproductions, varied by an occasional textile or dinner plate. The flower was king, although we never looked a real daffodil in the face. This compulsive pattern-making can be explained only by the preconception of our art master, a Welshman called Morgan: he was an opera singer in disguise who bloomed on Visitation Day when he sang Pagliacci in a borrowed tunic.

As my teachers were puzzled by my ineptitude in all other subjects (willing to learn though I clearly was) they initiated a prize for art when I left school so that I would have at least one success to alleviate my cheerless adolescence. I soon lost the prize book, but for years comforted myself with another stolen from my brother (whose initial is also M) and who did not miss one from his loaded prizes shelf.

As I moved through a fog of imperception towards adulthood only one thing was clear, at some point I would emerge from somnambulistic youth to become an ARTIST. My ambition was modest; there seemed to me then little, if any, difference between ART and COMMERCIAL ART, while the latter had at least the implication that, through it, I might avoid malnutrition.

I was inhibited by an incapacity to draw accurately, so as I trollied bales of silk to East End dressmakers and sold made-to-measure enamelled table tops to hygienic housewives, I spent anxious evenings at the Central School drawing the big toe of Greek casts and the plaster breasts of sexless goddesses, dreaming of the day when I might earn £3 a week in a few hours a day and be free to devote myself to the image of ART which I only barely comprehended and in the practice of which I was clearly incompetent.

I relate these sordid reminiscences only because they indicate that a passion for art is not necessarily dependent on understanding or ability. It can arise from a malfunction of the brain and a distortion of personality at least overtly independent of heredity or environment. At home art was a monochrome *Stag at Bay*, a porcelain Chinese mandarin with a nodding head, and an enlarged photograph of one of my eight Russian aunts which my mother used to pass off as herself when young. At school only the dog-eared Morris crib provided visual stimulation.

I will not burden you with the history of the chrysalis turning into an art-greedy moth, of the brain-sweeping by Fry, Bell, Wilenski and Read, of the vision of eternity which the National Gallery and the Tate disclosed, of the realisation in Paris that I could draw if I was concerned not with stylistic preconception or attempts to memorise, but was willing to achieve complete identity with the model or object I was examining with trance-inducing concentration.

I returned from Paris with 400 drawings, and the conviction that Commercial Art could only serve as a stomach filler while I reserved my energies for ART which I accepted with

Ark No 48 on Failure, Spring 1971.

masochistic dedication as my destiny. All the drawings, apart from three, got lost somewhere during the war, but the conviction remained unimpaired for many years as I transferred my allegiance from drawing to painting. This is a far cry from my present occupation of designing diesel locomotives and underground stations.

If this were the story of a single perambulation from art to design, it would have no more significance than the track left by an snail as it proceeds slowly from life to death, but my art-to-design transit is typical of many designers of my generation who believed that design was an aspect of art, that the creative energy of the artist could be subsumed by design and that to move from early experimentation in art to professionalism in design was to achieve success. I now believe it to be failure.

Design is not an uncreative and unsatisfying occupation, nor does it necessarily lack social justification. The failure lies in a restriction to the scaling of minor slopes when the capacity to reach at least the foothills of a mountain is believed to exist. Design I believe to be of less consequence than art as the Concorde is less significant than Rembrandt's self-portraits. Having reached this not very original conclusion at an age when death is closer than birth, when I have cotton-wooled myself with ingenious protective devices to dull the impact of conscious failure, my quietude has been shattered by the slogan-shouting of a new generation of student artists and the designers who again claim that art and design are inseparable parts of an art/design Siamese twin, and that those who attempt a dichotomy are barber surgeons who do not know the difference between a hair cut and an amputation. Alas, poor theory, I knew it well.

'Good design' as an ethical crusade

I find it difficult to believe that this indivisibility theory is based on the same faulty premises as those which motivated me in the early 1930s. Then 'good design' was an ethical crusade. My friends and I believed that Adolf Loos was right when he castigated decoration as evil, that the Bauhaus was a Vatican from which all truth emanated, and that good design could transform our environment and, in doing so, transform mankind. We found time to excuse deviation by the Russians from the narrow path of Platonic virtue, but did not waver from our conviction that GOOD design could be recognised, that it represented the forces of righteousness and that the Philistine hordes were typified by floral cretonnes and Turkish-type rugs.

The strength of these convictions turned painters into designers, sculptors into modellers of automotive bodies and me into an industrial designer. Fail safe it may have been as riding the crest of the initial wave of design popularity eventually turned penury into plenty, but a failure it has proved to be as I have become convinced that the concept of design as an aspect of art is unfounded. The success of the designers, limited though it be, has disclosed the flaws in the theories which sustained their original enthusiasm.

In the 1920s Corbusier could compare an automobile with the Parthenon; today this innocent reverence for the assumed non-aesthetic of the engineer has been exploded by the evidence that when engineers are concerned with the design of consumer products, they are influenced as much by personal predilections and marketing desiderata as by abstract concepts of efficiency-induced beauty. We have lowered our sights from the Parthenon to the market place and are content to compare car with car, television set with television set, plastic mug with mug.

For those involved in the retreat from self-confidence in their authority as artists to an acceptance that they are purveyors of elegant bijoux for pleasant places is an admission of failure on the grand scale.

The design of objects and systems is an estimable occupation. It requires technical knowledge and skills, mechanical and formal inventiveness, visual and tactile sensitivity, an understanding of human needs and an awareness of the structure of society manifest in the symbolism which generates fashion and is eventually characterised by style. When the objects are hand made they can exceptionally be expressive and of the same order as art; when they are mass produced they can be useful, agreeable and sometimes as elegant as a mathematical equation. Those who have the ability to be creative within what Bronowski has called the triangle of forces, of materials, production processes and use can find personal fulfilment in this occupation, but those who have once set their sights at Cezanne's apples or Picasso's Demoiselles get little satisfaction from designing a London bus or an Olivetti typewriter.

The art syndrome still plagues the designers. It makes them look for qualities which cannot exist within the boundaries of their undertaking; it sets them chasing after fine words to butter their epicurean parsnips. Those who aimed to be artists and have turned out to be designers must renounce manqués. They must take pleasure in moulding the form of an electric kettle instead of carving a Pieta.

Students will be quick to identify this special pleading as the self-pity of the old, the beating of the penitent's hoary chest. The design students' moral problems now arise not from their questioning of the validity of the act of design, but from their assessment of the social value or uselessness of the objects or systems for which they are partially responsible.

The failure of the artist-turned-designer is a 1930s hang-up. The problem is now transposed: it is that of the artist who sometimes believes that he can simultaneously be both expressive as an artist and rational and objective as a designer, that the creative aspects of design can be separated from its technical matrix, and that the artist can make a design contribution without participation in basic technical development.

This, admittedly, he can exceptionally do, but fashionable Formgebung and decoration is the normal outcome of the art/design mix, argued for with passionate conviction by

58

some art students. When the artist turns designer he ceases to be an artist, if one is to judge art by achievement at its peaks. It could be argued that this is for the good. Better a competent designer than a second-rate painter or sculptor; certainly let the artist turn designer, if he so wishes, but let us not confuse the transient values of design with the fundamental qualities of art.

The schism between art and design

If I believe, as I do, that a schism exists between art and design, should I admit that my continuing to occupy a professorial chair in the Royal College of Art is another example of the frailty of my character, of a failure to act in accordance with my principles? I do not consciously believe it is so. There is an advantage in co-existence and dubiety. The cohabitation of artists and designers of the same institution helps to create the unease, friction and tension which is essential to creative undertakings. Other advantages flow from the Victorian misconceptions which placed art and design education under the same academic and administrative authority.

Only exceptionally are students of the fine arts or of design geniuses; a few will eventually produce work of impressive quality; the majority will become competent technicians with a modest quota of creativity. Given the chance they will serve the community well, as do architects, surgeons, engineers and prison visitors. At the level of creativity at which most students work, the division between the fine arts and design is indistinct. The emphases and techniques are different, but the objective becomes identical – the production of objects which embellish our environment. It is no wonder that many of the middlemass artists who realise that they lack genius try to break through their picture frames to participate in environmental experiments.

The designers, conscious of the restrictions within which their creativity can be demonstrated, find solace in their physical association with the student painters and sculptors who proclaim the essential utility of the useless. Each is the salt in the other's wound. On the central plateau of inventiveness and competence, art and design students share equally the pleasure and anguish of creative experiment. The propinquity of many disciplines proves the opportunity for interchange and at least partially obliterates the spectre of isolation.

At the extreme polarity of genius, art and design are as different as fire and water, but all that any academic institutions can do for genius is to provide shelter, warmth and an efficient canteen.

I have left until last the exploration of the lesser shores of failure. I have known a few designers who are pleased with their work, not only while they are doing it but even when it is completed. This enviable self-satisfaction has eluded me as it does most who at some stage in their careers have been more intent on innovation than on refinement and consolidation. Every design project when completed discloses its imperfections; it cannot be more than an indicator of a better solution.

The designer is pursued by failure. Only momentarily does he take pleasure in a present achievement before he is again harassed by the realisation of how far short it falls of the initial concept. The anguish is multiplied when the designer works for industry when almost without exception the design concept is vitiated as it is sifted through committee decision and manufacturing and marketing restraints. In this sense the working life of any creative designer is one of accumulating failures, of partial successes which are only tolerable in the retrospect of photographs carefully taken to exaggerate the good and minimise the execrable.

The most oppressive aspects of the sense of guilt by failure are, I hope, restricted to my generation of artist-turned-designer. They spring from Platonic concepts of ideal solutions to problems of content and form which thus carry within their formulation the certainty of failure. It is now clear, or should be, that all industrial design is ephemeral and disposable; it is concerned with an expendable aesthetic, it can be as exciting as designing a new automobile or cigarette pack, or as useful as participating in the design of a system for mass urban transportation or hospital refuse disposal, but it is always concerned with solutions to immediate social/aesthetic/environmental problems and should be judged only in relation to immediacy and not against more exacting criteria. The job done should be filed away, and not carried through life as a burden of mal-achievement.

The artist, who is concerned with the fundamentals of life and death, love and hatred, ecstasy and misery, is allowed the lugubrious consolation of pessimism, but the designer must believe in the social value of his task – at least momentarily while he is working at it. No wonder, therefore, that many designers yearn for commissions with SOCIAL PURPOSE: throughout the world industrial design students are working on toys for crippled children, equipment for the handicapped, and artificial limbs which, if they were manufactured, would exceed the need.

"The essential characteristic of the designer is an unquenchable optimism..."

If people mutate, why should not the objects they desire or believe they need equally twist and turn, change and counterchange in an unceasing gavotte? The essential characteristic of the designer is an unquenchable optimism, and as often as not the ability to anaesthetise his intellect to allow for momentary belief in the validity of his task.

I do not, in fact, question the validity of designing a still more elegant and economic disposable cigarette lighter or of a yet more efficient and hygienic fully automated hospital food-preparation system. The importance of the form of a knife and fork or a television set is not diminished by the war in Vietnam, homelessness in Britain or floods in Pakistan, but it is no longer possible to delude oneself that political acquiescence is justified by professional activity.

In the meanwhile, I take irresponsible consolation in the knowledge that what I have designed is my personal graffito and that jobs still to be done will occupy my time until the final personal failure of death itself.

Craft : Art or Design?

Sir Misha Black

Lecture to the Institute of Craft Education, Northampton, April 1976

Three graduates of the Fine Arts from Leeds Polytechnic, *The Times* recently reported, walked 150 miles in East Anglia with a 10-foot yellow pole tied to their heads. When asked why they did it, one of the three, Raymond Richards, replied: 'It is an attempt to tread new ground in the art world.'

The August 1975 issue of the Italian magazine *Domus* described Christo's 'Running Fence'. It is: '...a barrier six meters tall and thirty kilometres long in a landscape outside San Francisco which crosses fourteen roads, a small town, a highway and a state road. The Running Fence project has an impact on people's lives because one of its foundations is irrationality'. In the same issue of *Domus*, a full colour page was devoted to an exhibition by Arman at the John Gibson gallery in New York.

Arman comes on, wearing boots and gloves and protected by large spectacles and armed with an axe, a sledge hammer and shears. In seventeen minutes the family hearth, symbol of the conventional dream of the immigrant avid for security, has become a battlefield, a refuse bin, a night-soil dump after the slaughter. The black angels have passed this way.

I have recorded these contemporary art forms not to deprecate them, but as examples of the dissolution of the matrix which contained the visual arts for five millenniums. It is as though the bones of a man had disintegrated, and muscles, organs and blood alone were trying to re-create its form.

Conceptual, Minimal and Performance Art are not the only manifestations of contemporary art nor even the most prolific, but they are, I believe, virile in expressing the anguish and disillusion which characterises the work of many young artists. It is work which I think I understand, although for which I have no sympathy. One cannot love one's own executioner.

The common factor in work of this kind is the attempt to smash through the barriers which separate art from its understanding by the majority of people. In the words of one young art student, the art which fills the London galleries is '...a phoney product of a phoney conditioned mind. It exists as a luxury of the bourgeois elite. It is totally irrelevant to the lives and the struggles of the great mass of the population'.

There is a connection between what I have said and the theme of this talk. I believe that the work of the Conceptual and Performance artists (when it is not itself phoney and an excuse for incompetence or social irresponsibility) is serious but misguided. It is a valiant foray down a blind alley. In attempting to find common ground for understanding, it surrounds itself with a smoke screen of self-deception. Support for it comes not from the masses which it attempts to reach but from the bourgeoisie which it purports to despise. The common ground will be found through the crafts, through the making of artefacts which, in fulfilling their practical or purely aesthetic purpose, reflect the ethos and style of the society which they celebrate. They express, or should express, those elements in our social structure which are humane and constructive. The whole of our social system is not evil. We should build with painstaking care on what has successfully been achieved by democracy, rather than risk the frail chance of reconstruction from the ruin produced by nihilism.

Nihilism and craftsmanship are not normally compatible. It is only when the craftsman is employed in the manufacture and embellishment of weapons of terror and destruction that compatibility occurs, but this is an aberration which we must subtract from generality. Craftsmanship is normally concerned with the making of objects for use, for adornment, for worship or for play. The man or woman who spends long hours carving wood or stone, building a chair or throwing and glazing a pot is far removed from the artist who destroys with an axe to demonstrate his disgust with those aspects of our society which justify his horror and despair.

Craft work is a reaffirmation of social value, if we should ever lose our sense of purpose in making as well as we can, society as we know it will be extinguished. High standards of craftsmanship are not, in themselves, the guarantee of social well-being. Perfection without purpose can be as negative as purpose without perfection, but if we lose the will to make as perfectly as we can all is certainly lost and nothing gained. I enjoy the privilege of a connection with the British Museum. It is a repository of perfection. An hour spent there reaffirms one's belief in the human race. Objects which can generate aesthetic pleasure hundreds of years after they have been made justify man's presumption of his being of the same substance as the gods he worships.

We should, however, distinguish between the making which produces not only an artefact but, simultaneously, a work of art. The utility object can give pleasure to its user as an efficient tool satisfies its operator, but for it to become a work of art, be it minor or major, another ingredient is essential.

This has been clearly expressed by Susanne K. Langer in her seminal book *Feeling and Form*.

> There is a definite reason to say a craftsman *produces* goods, but *creates* a thing of beauty; a builder *erects* a house, but *creates* an edifice if the house is a real work of architecture, however modest. An artefact as such is merely a combination of material parts, or a modification of a natural object to suit human purposes. It is not a creation, but an arrangement of given factors. A work of art, on the other hand, is more than an 'arrangement' of given things – even qualitative things. Something emerges from the arrangement of tones or colours (or forms) which was not there before, and this, rather than the arranged materials, is the symbol of sentience.

What Susanne Langer is writing about is the ineffable quality which distinguishes a Sung bowl from kitchen utensils, a Chippendale chair from a draughtsman's stool. It is what Matisse has described as 'an inherent truth which must be disengaged from outward appearance'.

Making does not necessarily produce art, but art cannot be produced without making. The unpainted picture, the unthrown pot, the unbuilt violin are illusions to pacify the paranoiac. They have no more substance than a day dream, a compensation of sorts for personal inadequacy.

Education by craft

I consider the crafts to be central to education. If craft is a vehicle for creativity and if creativity alone can provide the sense of well-being which will calm aggression, which I believe to be so, then education which excludes the crafts neglects one of its primary functions.

The role of art in education is now generally accepted, the expressive work of young children decorate and enrich most school rooms, but I believe there is an important distinction between teaching art (or rather allowing children the freedom to enjoy expressive activity) and education through craft work. The difference is that of technique.

Children's art, as it is brilliantly analysed in Herbert Read's *Education through Art*, is almost entirely an instinctive process. When the restraints of our social system are removed, most children, as most primitive people, draw and paint with spectacular effect. All that is needed is a degree of encouragement to break free from parental oppression (when this exists), the provision of paper and paints and off the children go to express their inner world and their reaction to their outer environment as though they were momentarily transformed from dreary drones into creative cherubs. That expressive art work is now the norm in most British schools is probably the most important development in education during the past 50 years. But it is not, in itself, enough.

Only a minority of children carry their early natural creativity into adolescence. Sensitive education in the crafts could bridge the gap between initial spontaneous child creativity and an older capacity for innovation.

Crafts must be taught and this can only be done by teachers who have themselves mastered one or more of the crafts. I exclude the simple manipulation of clay and plastic materials which are an aspect of early creativity, but if the older children are to work in a wood, metal or fabric workshop they must be taught how to use tools, how to make what they have conceived, how to temper creativity by patience. It is the last capacity which is perhaps the most difficult and most important to cultivate. Craftsmanship requires the ability to keep the pulse of creativity beating slowly over long periods. No one can build a spinet in a day or carve a stone frieze in a week.

I do not assume that every child, or in fact more than a very small proportion of them, will carry their initial capacity for creativity into adolescence, but if they are taught a craft they will at least retain the lesser satisfaction of being able to make things and enjoy the minor pleasure which is its inevitable concomitant. The exceptional few will find that their craft knowledge provides the essential matrix for real creativity, the creativity which gives distinction to the woodcarving in medieval churches, and transmutes a cycladic pot. The few who add creativity to skill will discover, through the discipline which making imposes, the key to unconscious knowledge which adds dimension to their conscious experience. When their work achieves the stature of greatness they will have drawn also on the inherent experience of the society to which they belong and which their work expresses.

The majority will be content to copy what already exists infrequently adding minor technical improvement and innovation. They will participate in the slow accumulative process which gradually, sometimes over many decades, modifies the form of artefacts which are largely made by hand with the assistance of tools which are themselves an extension of human dexterity. I have shifted my polemic ground from craft work which produces objects which are intended to be loved, hated or tolerated, as subjects for contemplation and overt aesthetic gratification, to those in which practicality predominates; from jewellery to saddles. I have done so intentionally because there is no precise dividing line between pleasure and use. Craft work is a broad spectrum of human activity. The magic which produces aesthetic empathy varies in different societies and in different epochs. The simple utility object of one society becomes the cherished museum treasure of another. The bark cloth of Polynesia and the sun-shielding hunting hats of the Eskimos are now as carefully conserved as the Great Gold Buckle of Sutton Hoo or the treasures of Tutankhamun.

Continuity or revolution

In November 1961, Herbert Read gave the Design Oration of the Society of Industrial Artists and Designers. He titled it 'Design and Tradition'. It was a passionate plea for the re-establishment of humanism in Western Society.

'The traditional concept of education is represented by the word humanism', he wrote. 'Humanism is the name given to the idea embodied in our Western tradition of education. It was felt by the originators of this tradition that whatever place the child would occupy in the world when it had grown to manhood or womanhood, its fitness to occupy that place with ability, and perhaps with distinction, would depend on basic qualities of character. Education was therefore designed for wholeness – for a uniform development of the mind and the body, of manners and accomplishments, of all those faculties that together would make the pupil a good and useful member of a peaceful and progressive society.' 'That idea', he continued, 'perished from the impact of two social revolutions. . . .'

I shall try later to relate this aristocratic concept to the problem of teaching at schools in a deprived working-class area, but let me first question his assumption that the effect of the two social revolutions, by which I assume he meant the industrial revolution and subsequently the social effects of the First World War, were wholly detrimental.

We must accept that human progress, by which I mean change and not necessarily improvement, is not smooth development but progresses as a series of jerks, by what Karl Marx described as 'thesis; antithesis; synthesis'. The industrial revolutions almost completely destroyed craft work as it existed in the eighteenth century and previously, but it found its antithesis in the resurgence of the arts and crafts movement of the mid-nineteenth and early twentieth centuries.

It is difficult now to sympathise with Adolf Loos' hysterical denouncement of decoration. 'The evolution of culture', he wrote in 1908, 'is synonymous with the removal of ornament from utilitarian objects. I believed that with this discovery I was bringing joy to the world; it has not thanked me'.

Eleven years later Walter Gropius issued his proclamation attempting again to assert the supremacy of the crafts. 'Architects, sculptors, painters, we must all return to the crafts! ...Painters and sculptors become craftsmen again, smash the frame of salon art that is round your pictures, go into the buildings, bless them with fairy tales of colour, chisel ideas into the bare walls' . . .

I hope you will excuse this minor historical diversion, but it is useful to remember the heroic periods when young men and women felt about craft work with the passion which we must now re-engender. Those who are teachers could make a vital contribution to the well-being of the next generation if they could inculcate their pupils with the conviction that to make is as important as to think, to express through making the ineffable qualities which only a rare few can transmute into speech.

The future of the crafts

I do not visualise all craft work as a striving to produce works of art. For a minority, craft techniques can be vehicles for pure creative activity only marginally, if at all, related practicality. For many, craft abilities can, throughout adulthood, be a source of pleasure in private achievement, but I hope that for a measurable number craft in education could open a door to work-a-day employment in which success and pleasure is not calculated only in cash returns. There is a desperate need for craftsmen in the building industry. Bernard Feilden (the architect to York Minster and St. Paul's Cathedral) has estimated that Britain is 4000 short of skilled specialised craftsmen for essential restoration work. Robin McCall (Secretary of the Association of Metropolitan Authorities) has calculated that the shortfall is 10,000 craftsmen needed for the retention and protection of our architectural heritage. We need blacksmiths for making railings, screens and wrought iron work; wood carvers; stonemasons; joiners and painters and many other craftsmen who can bring back to the building industry the skills which previously have been handed down from one generation to another and are now in danger of extinction.

For those who are prepared to undertake a longer period of study and apprenticeship there is work to be done in the conservation departments of museums and art galleries throughout the world.

It may be that if craftsmen again become available the architects may find work for them in new building to provide the enrichment which now is sadly lacking from most contemporary structures.

Craft and industrial design

I have left until towards the end an attempt to relate craft work to modern industry. In Herbert Read's oration, from which I have already quoted, he wrote: 'The sensibility that coursed along the nerves and veins of countless generations of craftsmen must be made to flow again in the veins and nerves of our industrial designers.' 'Sensibility' is the missing factor. It is manifest, without conscious endeavour, in some works of engineering conceived at the frontiers of knowledge, it requires conscious decision when a myriad of alternatives present themselves to the designer for selection.

When the alternatives proliferate without increase of cost or reduction in efficiency the designer's decision is aesthetic. He draws the line where he will because it gives him aesthetic satisfaction, he relates plane to plane and form to form to produce relationships which satisfy an inexpressible sense of what is 'right'. His work is dignified by style. The industrial designer thus works very much in the same way as does the artist-craftsman. He perceives a desired end, but in working towards it, he changes course, probes the unconscious depth of his knowledge and understanding, and sometimes succeeds in producing a result which, in Oscar Wilde's words, is 'both surface and symbol'.

The industrial designer needs to learn the craft of model-making so that he can test his concept against a mock reality while the design takes shape. He differs from the traditional craftsman because his final model is not the thing in itself but an analogue of the end product. His models and drawings and specifications are instructions to be communicated to the machines, but nevertheless his creative process is comparable to that of the craftsman even if he must relinquish the special pleasure of personal accomplishment in which the handmark identifies a unique production.

Many boys and girls now enthusiastically assimilate technical instruction and it is tempting to introduce them also to the techniques of industrial design, so that their mechanisms achieve the gloss of finished marketable products. There is danger in this.

Teachers are adult and tend to be set in a pattern established in their childhood and youth. This creates its own sense of style. In previous epochs the teacher could be satisfied that the style appropriate to his generation would be valid, with only minor modification, to the next.

Now that patterns of social behaviour, of faith and judgement, change at accelerated pace, no one can be convinced that what was right for his generation can be an acceptable mode for the next. The craft teacher should therefore be content to teach the craft but not attempt to influence form. He or she should, however, use all their guiles and experience in trying to persuade their pupils to study the history of their craft whether it be jewellery or ceramics. The young craftsman may properly revolt against historical continuity, but the revolt itself is an aspect of the human continuum. Cruelty resides in allowing the child craftsman to work in the vacuum of no knowledge so that when he rediscovers the wheel his pleasure and self-confidence is later destroyed by the appreciation that he is not at the head of his time.

Learning to judge

The historical perspective is essential to an appreciation of the contemporary environment. Learning about craft is as important as learning through craft. It may be that most children can more easily comprehend history if it is learned backward, from the present to the past with gargantuan leaps over centuries, so that the social life of previous epochs, and the crafts which commemorate them are quickly appreciated in crude perspective. We must know how the people of other periods produced their man-made environment, where they succeeded and where they failed, so that we can measure our world against theirs.

If learning is consistently associated with making, this could be an approach to visual comprehension, to a visual sensitivity which could ennoble future generations. Eyes which see cannot tolerate the intolerable. Hand and eye need again to be linked in mutual understanding. The faint smoke signals which herald revolutionary fire are already visible. It is fanned by a hundred local amenity societies, it is manifest in a growing revulsion against much of post-war building, in a desire to achieve human scale where grandeur is not appropriate.

But the understandable reaction against the present results mainly in a desire for conservation. A standstill may be justified while we prepare for new construction in a style which more reasonably reflects the ambition of our society, but conservation alone is negative and can only, in the long term, result in atrophy.

We must recover the confidence which sustained craftsmen and builders in previous epochs. I believe that education through art, and education through craft, could produce in the future what my generation has singularly failed to achieve. If we teach children how to make and how to get pleasure from making they may eventually rediscover the magical formula which enables them also to make well.

Conclusion

This talk has, I fear, turned into a series of unstructured generalisations and for this I apologise, but I wanted only to affirm what I know you already believe, that the crafts should not be considered as a relaxation from the sterner stuff of academic study, but they should be at the centre of the educative process. They can be the bridge between those who have been capable of learning and deprived children who seek satisfaction only in the rebellion which destroys without building. In secondary education the arts and the crafts can relate knowledge to feeling and understanding. In adult life the capacity to make can be inspiration or solace.

The arts and crafts are not easy options. They require the capacity for facing ultimate truth, the truth which without self-deception enables one to know the difference between success and failure, which sees partial success as a stepping-stone towards greater understanding, and comprehends failure as a goad.

Bronowski wrote that the attribute of scientists is 'the habit of truth'. I believe this should also be true for those whose study is the humanities. Self-deception is the inexcusable crime. Craft work cannot be smudged over, there is no escape from the eyeball to eyeball confrontation when what is made looks at its creator and judges him as he judges his creation.

" I do not expect all craftsmen to be geniuses. It will suffice if they are truthful and humble."

I do not expect all craftsmen to be geniuses. It will suffice if they are truthful and humble, make as best they can for the glory of mankind and, in doing, so celebrate their own divinity.

The Harmonious Spark

Professor Richard Guyatt
Medallist 2000
Lecture given at the SIAD annual conference in 1976.
The theme of the conference was 'Head, Heart and Hand'.

When the late Robin Darwin was appointed as the new Principal of the Royal College of Art in 1948 and set about re-organising it from top to bottom, he offered me the new Chair of Publicity Design. While jumping at the job – Professors were to be paid £1,200 a year – I protested about the title. Partly, I suspect, from snobbish reasons but ostensibly for the far better reason that such a title would restrict unduly the courses that I felt my School should run. I wanted the School, though centred on advertising, to range more freely through other graphic areas. Luckily for me *The Times* came out at that moment with an article on the reorganisation of the College and frowned, en passant, at the need for such a title as Professor of Publicity. This turned the tables in my favour and I can remember sitting with Robin and wondering what alternative name we could dream up to call this new School. Eventually we decided on Graphic Design, a new and meaningless phrase in those days but one which suited my purpose, giving me ample room in which to construct new courses. I remember I veered towards 'School of Graphic Arts' (a title which the School has eventually achieved – but only last year) but Robin was so keen for the College to become known as a design school rather than an art school that he plumped for Graphic Design.

I made one other condition of appointment – that I was never, under any circumstances, to be expected to give a lecture. This was agreed, to my great relief, yet such was the Darwin charm, and skill in the gentle art of blackmail, that it wasn't long before I found myself forced to start preparing my Inaugural Lecture. I called it 'Head, Heart and Hand'. [and it was given at the Royal Society of Arts in 1950].

I have just re-read it – in the course of preparing this paper – for the first time since I delivered it over a quarter of a century ago and a strange experience it has proved to be. Yet I find that I stand by the principles which I attempted to formulate by writing it, and indeed they have stood me in good stead in the intervening years. If anything my belief in them has strengthened.

In that lecture I attempted to define the relationship between the fine arts, the applied arts, and the crafts. It was an ambitious undertaking and I learned much from the attempt. I started from the position that each of these divisions, or facets of art, could generate, each at their own level, a true creative process. The fine artist was not the only practitioner concerned with art, and indeed that a real work of art could well be a combination of all three.

If this were so, could the creative process itself be defined or analysed as the central activity giving rise to these various manifestations, to these various branches of art? I argued that this mysterious process was generated by emotional and intuitive feelings, that these feelings were modified and structured by intellectual analysis, and eventually given physical form, manifested through manual skill. From this I argued that if the central creative process was constructed by this 3-fold harmony, this 3-fold dance, then in the fine arts, with their poetic insights and intuitive understandings, the emotional element might be the central one, while with design, with its need to satisfy functional demands, this central role might shift to the intellect – to the pleasure of solving problems – and with the crafts the delight in manual skills might take the leading position. But in each case it was the delight, the pleasure, the attraction of the process which formed the harmonious spark which unites them to ignite this indefinable force called 'art'.

Although this may be true in a broad and general sense, I now feel that such a formulation is too clear cut, too neat and oversimplified, for I believe that at each level of art – be it fine art, design or craft – one can have an emotional, or an intellectual, or craft-based springboard. For example, we all know the difference between the meticulously precise, grid-bound, analytical Swiss typography, and the more relaxed, generous and intuitive typography practised over here. Yet it is the very delight in *precision*, on the one hand, and in *richness* on the other, which *equally* energises these differing approaches. And though artists and designers – like most normal people – are most probably equally developed in all these compartments of their nervous system, yet each individual practitioner has a predilection for one or other of its divisions – he is something of a 'head' man or a 'heart' man or a 'hand' man and this will condition the type of designs he will produce. Hence the importance, if one adopts this point of view, of knowing yourself.

I have frequently seen students, whose talents are clearly intuitive, yet who are so beguiled by the look of Swiss typography, or who have been told that this is the only way to do it, or who are just imitating a fashion, that they slog away producing poor imitations of a style of work which in fact is against their nature. Indeed the process of learning is to come to grips with one's own true talents, and to discover or uncover whatever they are. And I subscribe to the Platonic view that the teacher only plays the role of the midwife in this process of self-discovery.

And as another illustration of my thesis from a slightly different direction, I am aware, as I'm writing this, that I'm writing it with my head (helped by hand and my interest in the subject). But I am also aware that all this thought I have just formulated in words, can be intuitively felt and arrived at directly with great rapidity and with no need for a carefully thought-out intellectual formulation. Maybe it's much the better way for some people – certainly for me, for my mental make up finds 'thinking' tough going. I know, from long experience, that I'm much more of an intuitive man.

My brief was to set out the case for 'Heart'. I'm not at all sure that I am capable of doing this, for it is a slippery and elusive subject. As John Keats says in one of his letters to his brother, 'The Heart is the Mind's Bible, it is the Mind's Experience, it is the Text from which the Mind or Intelligence sucks its identity'. That perhaps, speaking metaphysically, is as close as we can get to the subject.

But it brings me to a point which has been interesting me a great deal recently. That is the extraordinary difference between the intangible, immaterial world of ideas, and the material, tangible world of fact and artefact. And how it is the immaterial world of ideas, of inspiration, which conditions the material world. How, in the terms of this paper, Head and Heart work at the intangible level while Hand manifests the artefact at the material level. I mean this quite simply. For example, I get the idea of building a conservatory onto my house, I 'see' it in my mind's eye and am entranced with the whole concept. If the right process is put in motion – lo and behold, in a few month's time there it is, in actual fact, looking quite like my visualisation, plucked as if by magic out of thin air – and bulging with real plants and flowers. Seen like this art proves to be a process for the manifestation of ideas and understanding, and perhaps this gives me the excuse to talk about the state of art and design as I see it after my long association with the Royal College.

In doing this it is interesting to try and recapture the climate of the day when I wrote that inaugural lecture. It was a 'short-back-and-sides' world. It was, of course, well before television and its commercials had us in their grip, before space travel and the idea of landing on the moon had been dreamed of, before the Festival of Britain (indeed I was working on the designs for my pavilion – the Lion and Unicorn – as I wrote that lecture), before motorways, well before The Beatles and Pop groups and Carnaby Street, before drip-dry shirts and mini-skirts. It was a world which was recovering, in a sober, rationed way, from the effects of the war, trying to re-establish a normality which had vanished forever – the life style of the 1930s.

In the arts, though the mood was for breaking up tradition, artists still used brushes and oil paint and canvas, and words like aesthetics could still be used and still had a meaning. The New York School, with Andy Warhol emerging out of Duchamp's' proposition that 'I am an artist, therefore anything I choose to do, or not to do, is a work of art,' had yet to establish itself as the leading influence and art students still wanted to visit Paris! It was another world. And the fine arts still held sway as the leaders of the hierarchy. They were the aristocrats and the pace setters.

I'm not so sure that this is so today. In the intervening years there have been so many experiments, so many new movements, so much search for originality, so many minimal ops and pops, that they appear to have dissipated their aim and to have become something of a bore – obscure in their elitism. Who can, in truth get anything much from a conceptual artist's exhibition? It takes a very special talent and knowledge. And with the blurring of the boundaries between the various art forms, audio-visual techniques of impact on the hapless onlooker are bewildering and mystifying. But are they enriching? Perhaps to that minority in the 'know'.

However that may be, I have long subscribed to the idea that the arts must be the servants of some inspiring force other than themselves. I'm no Art for Art's sake man, and from even a superficial knowledge of history it is abundantly clear, past need of proof, that some of the most sublime manifestations of the work of artists, architects and craftsmen are concerned with the various religions which energised the different civilisations at different periods and in different parts of the world – be it Greece or China, India or Egypt, Mexico or Europe. Art has always been a channel for this upsurge of the human spirit, and until relatively recently, say the seventeenth century in Europe, the arts and crafts have always centred round the religious forces of their place and time. They spoke to the Heart.

But in a period such as ours, when spiritual belief is dormant, and the great drive is for an ordered technology and material well-being, what are the arts to do? What are they to serve? One obvious answer is that they can serve society at the industrial and commercial level and we, as a collection of professional designers with many different specialisations, know how far ranging that front is. But speaking as an art teacher I know that that answer is naïve and over-simplified. It is speaking in the language of yesteryear – the language being spoken as an expression of the way we thought when the College was re-organised so long ago. Certainly amongst students today there is a strong urge to serve society, and this, alas, has largely taken the place of that search for aesthetic emotion, that search for a blend of the beautiful with the practical in design, which dominated my youth. But this urge to serve society does not necessarily mean to work for industry. Political and sociological stances come in to cloud the issue and not all students find the capitalist industrial system the ideal area in which to work. They would prefer to breathe the purer air of work based not on self-interest, but on altruism dedicated to the real needs of mankind, irrespective of the profit motive. They are naturally attracted to what are called 'anti-materialistic values'.

We recently staged an international Design conference at the Royal College called 'Design for Need' [which involved Misha Black]. It was a great success and very well attended, and some of the titles of the papers which were read and discussed illustrate the point I am trying to make.

For example: 'The Design of an Urban Transport System using the Ergonomic Approach'; 'A new Approach to the Design of Playsites and Playstructures'; 'Ergonomic Analysis of Personal Hygiene Activity and Equipment'; 'Designing for the Disabled: a new field of work'; 'Table-ware and Furniture for the Disabled'; 'The Design of Emergency and Disaster Equipment'; etc, etc.

I've picked these titles at random from the three-day programme but they give a pretty good picture of the sort of conference it was. It was certainly worthwhile, heavy with political overtones, and strongly aware of social responsibilities.

But I was left wondering about this word 'Design'. As used in this conference it was linked with engineering and construction technologies – and in fact any man-made object – I beg your pardon 'person-made object', the phrase used by a woman speaker at the conference – any object has in a sense got to be designed. But the 'design' I am interested in, and about which I am attempting to talk, is quite different, and is to do with the poetic significance – call it what you will – of the language of visual messages – and not with utility structures which have a totally different aim.

When Victor Papaneck designs wireless sets powered by cow dung for developing nations, I shouldn't think that what they look like rates very highly in his list of priorities. And he's quite right. He's not going after art, and his activity is most probably powered by compassion and his intellectual love of ingenuity.

And in this 'Design for Need' conference the speakers always took 'Need' at a material, social level – such as recycling waste products, disaster reliefs, alternative approaches to housing problems, etc. These are true and important needs and at some moments in history are more urgent and imperative than at others. But it is equally true that, coexisting with these needs and in a sense underlining them and underpinning them, there is also another need, a need for the enrichment of the spirit and a deepening of understanding. And this practice of art – be it fine art, design or craft – can be an approach to this, at many different degrees and levels from the merest folk art to works of profound genius.

Yet this search for a social *raison d'etre*, which takes the form of a political left wing stance, has spread to the fine art world. I can remember the day, not so long ago, when a young painter, if he were to have a successful career as an artist, had to have a smash hit Bond Street success before he was thirty. Not so today. Such a success is to be avoided at all costs! Dealers and critics are regarded as manipulators who create an elitist situation by building up and protecting individual artistic reputations in a search for the quick, though lasting capitalist buck. And it may well be that much that appears destructive, brutal and often ridiculous in the fine arts today, has as its aim the shaking up of society in an attempt to stand it on its head. At all events to shake off the past – that sticky fly-paper 'History' – and to start afresh.

This attempt to break with the past has been largely successful – peculiarly so in the visual arts. Ask students sitting for the College entrance exam what they think of the 'Old Masters' – say Rembrandt, Velásquez, Leonardo, Cezanne – the answer is usually, that today they are 'irrelevant'. (Some time ago now I asked a candidate what he thought of Goya and was baffled by his answer until I realised he thought I was talking of lip-stick! And this year I came across two candidates sitting the Illustration exam who had never even heard of Gustave Dore or Daumier.)

In a sense they are right – these great masters have little to say to the contemporary non-figurative, hard edged, conceptual, generation of fine art students. Yet I find it hard to believe that say Shakespeare, Milton, Cervantes or Tolstoy would be so dismissed by students of literature or that Mozart, Beethoven, Wagner or Chopin would fail to stir the respect of students of music. Perhaps I am wrong, but there seems to be to be a very clean break in the development of the visual, as opposed to the other, arts. It seems to me, but I plead great ignorance of literature or music, that visual art – that form of art which deals with making visual images by drawing, painting or sculpture – has been knocked off its traditional perch to a greater extent than the other arts, by the advent of a *technology*, in the guise of photography, the film and television. This has forced them, if not into making a completely new start, at least to alter direction dramatically. I feel that the experiments in contemporary music and writing, though seeming every bit as 'way out', have come from an inborn need to develop along new ways, searching out new techniques representative of today. But in the case of the visual arts they are a reaction to the advent of a totally different process of mechanical image-making which has pulled the carpet from under their feet and left them wondering what to do next and why do it?

At all events it is a bewildering and difficult time in which to be an art student. Originality is at a premium and this often results in painfully unsatisfactory ego trips. The frustrating search for a worthwhile aim, combined with the refusal to be part of a tradition, yet, at the same time, the 'comme-il-faut' need to be seen to be part of a contemporary movement, reduces the work of art students to a dull uniformity, flashed occasionally with brilliance. I suspect that throughout history this has always been the case – for whatever reason. For true talent is always rare and imitation is always rife.

I expect we've all read Tom Wolfe's 'emperor's clothes' article on modern art – *The Painted Word* – in a recent number of *Harpers & Queen*. And whatever you may think of the article – spiteful or revealing – I feel his main contention is valid – that, and I quote: 'Modern Art has become completely literary: the paintings and other works exist only to illustrate the text'. In other words, you have to understand the theory before you can see the picture. In terms of this paper there's too much 'Head' around in the studios and too little 'Heart' and this can be dangerously stultifying. In my own personal experience in the recent past, I've seen an extremely talented student – a really superb draughtsman – get so caught up in conceptual theories, getting so immersed in the meaning of words, that

72

he ground to a halt – and I believe has now taken up a form of conceptual photography. At all events, he doesn't draw any more.

And the present situation is summed up in a recent article by Richard Cork on the *Rokeby Venus* and the National Gallery. In it he writes:

> The nineteenth-century idea of the artist as an independent miracle-worker, unconstrained by the need to satisfy a patron's whims and rising above the demands of a philistine public still dominates our thinking today.

The whole concept of a museum full of identically displayed trophies, each one ripped out of its initial context and preserved like an isolated specimen of an *inexplicable* activity called *art* only fosters the *mistaken* belief that artists are rarefied beings who have no easily definable place in our society. Far from liberating them, such a notion castrates artists by denying them any practical efficacy and exhorting them to view their activities as an enclosed discourse, of interest only to aesthetes and educated specialists...'

But things are different when we come to consider that level of art called design. Here is an art-form which is constrained by satisfying 'a patron's whims' and which has to take into account 'the demands of a philistine public'. Standing firm and uncastrated the designer does not view his activities as 'an enclosed discourse'. Only the trouble is that these very constraints, so laudable from a certain point of view, pin down a designer to work at a certain level – a wholesome level, but one not calculated to stimulate the highest and most penetrating aesthetic insights.

But then in the long run society gets the arts it asks for – in some ages religious, in some ages secular, in some political, in ours, for the most part, commercial. And this is not to be wondered at in a period when man spends his energies and resources in vast technological enterprises such as the miracle of landing people on the moon. Today we live in a period unlikely to foster the highest forms of art, for its loves and its proclivities lie elsewhere – for the time being.

But though this may be true, speaking philosophically and on a large scale, the practical issues remain on our own personal scale as individual artists. Creative energies lie within each one of us and how can we make the best of them? What a question! And how can it possibly be answered? And yet some consideration of it could be well worthwhile, for the fascination of following this profession, of being an artist, is that it implies (unlike some other professions) the possibility of a continuous development of one's own powers throughout one's life. This may be optimistic of me. and I'm well aware that talents dry up, getting stale and rigid. Yet I believe the reverse is also true and I'm certainly not one to believe that everything is for the young! Their particular delight is in their promise – but this can also be a difficult cross to bear.

Let us return to our initial proposition that the creative process is energised by the harmonious interplay and balance of the three aspects of man's make-up – Head, Heart and Hand. I believe this interplay comes about more easily after long practice in the relaxed sureness of maturity. One knows what one's up to, one has great interest in doing it, and one has the skill to pull it off. But the delight in doing it must remain – if that spark, that harmonious spark is extinguished then talents wither and lose their inner creativity.

And though each individual designer must find the aim of his work in the disposition and development of his talents, yet he must also find a worthwhile role within the society in which he works. Clearly a designer – be he a product designer or a decorative one – helps the wheels of industry go round. But what is more significant and particular is that he is able to do this through his response and sensitivity to the appearance of the world around him, at that material level I referred to earlier. This in a designer, can trigger off the immaterial level of ideas and understanding, enriching him and his work. This is his hall-mark and his peculiar talent, that the look of things 'turn him on', be they man-made or natural, and this enables him to talk their language and understand them. He is uniquely constituted, therefore, to enrich society in this *particular* way. This must be his main role, to be a channel through which more beauty and delight can be brought to Society, to enliven it and to bring civilising influences, at as many different levels and in as many different ways as possible – from the severely practical to the aesthetically significant. Too much ugliness has appeared in our society of late, helped alas by designers, in the name of progress, technology, function or expediency. But perhaps the pendulum will begin to swing the other way and aesthetics will be given the importance which they once held.

This for me is surely the root of the matter, that artists, designers and craftsmen, by practising their own skills, should, by the quality of their work, increase the spiritual wellbeing of society – without which there can be little material wellbeing. This must be the aim, and speaking personally my heart lies in it.

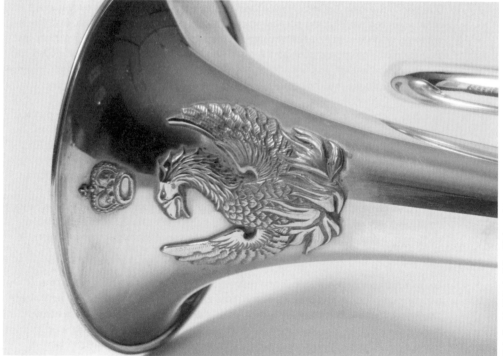

Phoenix, Richard Guyatt, 1967, on RCA Convocation Trumpet.

Photo: Dominic Tschudin © Royal College of Art

A People-based Approach

Professor Michael Twyman
Medallist 2014

In my address on the occasion of the Sir Misha Black Award ceremony I tried to explain what I held to be important in graphic design education. Among other things, I pointed to the value of design courses as a means of educating the whole person. I had in mind a specific field of design, typography and graphic communication, but I believe the point to be valid for design courses in general. Indeed, if you turn the argument on its head and look for a course capable of developing a wide range of abilities and skills in the individual – creative, visual, intellectual, manual, technical, social, cultural, managerial – what better possibilities can there be than one that focuses on design?

I ended by saying that my essential views about design education had not changed substantially over a period of some fifty years, despite all the scientific, technological and social changes that had taken place. Out of context this must seem thoroughly anti-progressive. But these views have to be seen in relation to some constants, and particularly that of the physiology of human beings. It is surely this that explains why many designed objects, and certainly the most commonly used ones, have remained essentially the same over the above period, and some of them over centuries. But would I be able to say the same thing about design education fifty years on, were I to be around? I have asked myself this question, but past experience tells me that I am not very good at predicting the future.

One thing does still seem clear. Education in design must aim to develop a broad range of skills in students if it is to meet one overriding requirement: to provide everyone with the means to adapt to change. This has always been important in education, but in such a fast moving world it is surely the priority. After all, some present-day students may still be working in fifty years time. For this reason I believe that design education should not be rooted exclusively in the present, either in its current technologies or its prevailing fashions. Clearly it must have a close relationship to the world of the day, whatever that is like. But in addition to providing students with a variety of generalisable skills for a different and unknown future, it should surely also look back at the rich cultural heritage of design. It has been said before, and by wiser heads than mine, that to look forward we need to know where we have been.

So it seems sensible to abandon predictions and fall back on a list of broad hopes for the future. The overriding issue in design education for me is that it should have the needs and aspirations of *people* at its core. This ought to be so now and must surely be so in the future if design education is to flourish. (I should perhaps make it clear that I am not making a distinction here between the needs and aspirations of people and any future developments in robotics and artificial intelligence.) By stating that people should be put at the core of design education I am simply arguing for two things: an education system that focuses on the needs of the individual student, and design courses that prioritise the needs of human beings and the societies in which they live.

It may seem self evident that the individual should be the focus of all education, and in recent years there has certainly been a growing acceptance that education should be

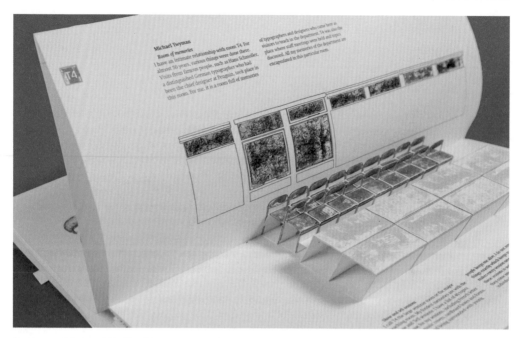

Book spread designed by Aline Geuquet as part of a Professional Practice Assignment, Department of Typography & Graphic Communication, Reading University.

student-centred. But that is not exactly what I mean: to some extent well-intentioned efforts to focus on the needs of students are counterproductive because they also tend to be constraining. I hope that design education programmes in the future would be more tolerant of those who feel the need to break out and do their own thing, even occasionally to fall foul of the system. But how is this to be catered for in an uncertain and challenging world where the pressure to conform looms so large?

There is also the question of motivation, of both students and teachers. Students are likely to be motivated or inspired by a variety of things: the challenge of problem-solving; the prospect of fame or business success; the achievements of notable designers; the opportunity to change society; a lively learning environment and enlightened teachers. But what of staff motivation? My hope would be that teachers are freed from many of the constraints stemming from those who administer education, thus allowing more scope for bottom-up innovation. This may mean paying far less attention to the structure of courses, assessment procedures, and the often rather bureaucratic systems of feedback, so that teachers are in a better position to explore their interaction with students in mutually beneficial ways. Motivating students and staff in the future will not be easy, particularly with the prospect of even larger teaching groups, shorter courses, more recourse to distance learning, and the deadening hand of top-down management. But it is a priority if design education, which has had a proud history of innovation and idealism, is to flourish in the future.

The other people-based approach to design education that I hope will be explored more in the future has to do with the issues that courses choose to address. Should the focus be on glamorous design problems, or on design that contributes in small, incremental ways to improving the world around us? What should we be doing about preparing students to address the needs of a rapidly growing elderly population? How do we communicate complex messages about such things as health, safety, legal matters to a diverse range of people from different language groups? And what part should the interests of the commercial world play in influencing what is taught? Inevitably, by emphasising certain issues and defining projects in particular ways, courses and teachers shape the local and global design agenda. Most obviously this relates to practical teaching and the choice of projects, but it even applies to the way in which we choose to interpret the history of design.

A people-based approach to design education would surely benefit from what used to be called 'design participation', that is, having designers solve problems alongside those who are going to be affected by the outcome. Some fields of design seem better disposed to such an approach than others, but faced with hard decisions, and particularly the temptation to follow resource streams, such crucial approaches to design tend to get neglected. When designers are locked into their machines and have almost everything under their control, there is a strong temptation to ignore external matters, such as discussion with and feedback from users. Design participation, though difficult to foster in an educational context, would greatly help to inculcate good design practice in the future.

"So much learning comes from physical experiences, like drawing, the use of tools, and three-dimensional manipulation."

I would also want to put in a plea for the greater encouragement of manual skills in design education. I believe that they need to be highlighted because so much learning comes from physical experiences like drawing, the use of tools, and three-dimensional manipulation. It seems to me that there is already a danger that such avenues of learning are being lost. The hope, therefore, is that all future design courses will include some aspect of brain to hand coordination, beyond that needed to operate a keyboard or mouse.

Happily, there is plenty of evidence that students are concerned about the future, and particularly what they see as the wrongs or ills of society, among them issues that affect the future of our planet. Some would surely relish the chance to play their part in solving these problems, and it could be argued that projects focusing on such issues are just as demanding and just as useful in promoting appropriate design procedures as those of the commercial world that most, in time, will surely enter. Faced with market forces in virtually every walk of life, including education, might it be time for design education to re-engage with some other needs of people? And can we hope for design manifestos in the next fifty years of the kind that there have been in the past?

Becoming Navigators

Professor David Crow

Award 2012

Edited abstract of a paper entitled 'Re-make, re-model' (2016), published by Joe McCullagh, Jane McFadyen, David Crow, Alan Holmes and Jane McKeating

Design practice constantly adapts to the context it finds itself in. Arguably, design practice also shapes the context itself, leading our thinking on a debate around a wide set of social and economic values that affect us all. Most recently this re-evaluation has led us to an understanding of design practice that needs to be embedded in a curated team, working alongside a diverse range of experts. Crucially designers are no longer confined to a single area of practice and work freely across disciplines and processes creating diverse conceptual outputs.

In 2008, the Museum of Modern Art New York exhibition, 'Design and the Elastic Mind', captured this shift by focusing on the ability of designers to 'grasp momentous advances' in nano-technology, science and human behaviour through translating those advances into functional human-centred designed objects and systems. Simultaneously we have seen a growing culture of design do-it-yourself (DIY), where self-authorship in design has emerged and where design is participatory as a social communal event with like-minded individuals in a design counterculture. Design is on the move from a service model to one that is increasingly event and scenario based.

Design and the Elastic Mind, MoMA New York, 2008.

The designer now engages in a whole new world of participatory engagement, becoming navigators, 'designers find themselves at the centre of an extra-ordinary wave of cross-pollination'[1] dealing with open ended customised solutions, where the user in effect takes a more participatory role. Sociological shifts towards a participatory practice in utilising social media have also enabled learners to become multimodal, strategically working across distributed knowledge economies where learning by default is a social process.

Student as 'navigator' is something that educators have had to respond to within our learning and teaching strategies. The recent wave of rebuilding the physical environment of our institutions has given many of us the opportunity to provide a 'social learning

---

[1] Antonelli, P. and Aldersey-Williams, H. (2008) The Museum of Modern Art, New York, Design and the Elastic Mind, (New York)

space' and the outcomes have been varied. Our attempts to translate this into the learning environment have in some cases been truly experimental whilst others have been little more than introducing social furniture into a traditional studio and distributing computers into libraries. As a catalyst for a new model of learning and teaching it has been refreshing and fascinating if not always successful. The idea of exclusive ownership of an entire curriculum alongside exclusive ownership of space are difficult to support alongside changes in the contemporary professional workplace and an increasingly international cultural context.

One could question the proposition that concentrating learning within the boundaries of the institution is sustainable. Bringing teams of students together to explore new ways of doing and making will require a flexibility about the ownership of our curricula, our processes and our structures. Constantly adding new content to existing curricula, within existing methodologies and conventional approaches to space will not cope with either the growing demand in creative arts education or the future professional needs of our students. As Wenger considers,

"What if we assumed that learning is as much part of human nature as eating and sleeping?"

… what if we adopted a different perspective, one that placed learning in the context of our lived experience of participation in the world? What if we assumed that learning is as much part of our human nature as eating or sleeping, that it is both life-sustaining and inevitable, and that – given a chance – we are quite good at it?[2]

Driven by changes in the socio-cultural, economic, political and the technological, and by the perceived danger of growing tired and self-referential, we all recognise there is a need to constantly re-make and re-model design education. Significantly there is a desire to create a design education culture which is truly flexible, responsive, adaptable, and where design becomes more integral to our lives and more accountable to those around us. To do this we need to enhance opportunities for multi-disciplinary working practices and collaborative relationships. We can also positively empower design education through forging a strong identification with its locale. Our locale is geographic where it is connected to a sense of place and also metaphoric, where our locale is another set of disciplines that also engage in design thinking and making. With this comes an emphasis on the transformational effect design can bring when we work as teams and a genuine sense of agency in our communities. To achieve this, we need to allow ourselves to reframe our role as educators and deliberately unlearn some of the practices that we have relied on for so many years. We could do worse than to start by looking to our own students whose fundamental approach is one of curiosity and inquiry – whilst having the confidence to attempt to deal with uncertain and complex situations.

[2] Wenger, E. (1998) Communities of Practice: Learning, Meaning and Identity (Cambridge: Cambridge University Press)

Where All Things Are Always Possible

Penny Macbeth and Joe McCullagh
Award 2012

'Design education is a place where all things are always possible... we are committed to how creativity and the transformative ability of design education changes lives for the good.'

Design education at the art school is about explorative experiences where the language of design is questioned, extended and applied; we are curious people and are always explorers...

'This all sounds quite interesting with plenty of education rhetoric, however...

What about the future? Isn't the future now, the present is not a permanent fixed point? What about the imminent danger of the extinction of design? Where lands will be occupied with roaming 'Designosaurs', scrambling for work. The real threat and role of artificial intelligence in the creative process and robots that make and produce design work. The ever-increasing use of algorithms driving market intelligence in determining public taste and design. Plastic fossils: designers will be asked to question the use of materials in a post-anthropocene era, where we question the origins of the materials we use, the waste they create and how as designers and innovators we have an opportunity and responsibility to rethink design ecologies. All of this set within a UK and arguably world politics that is in a state of flux in a period of uncertainty.'

'Good point; we'll try to stop making sense, we should therefore consider...'

The blurring of the virtual and physical

The further distorting of the virtual and physical will enable design to reshape. As our world becomes further networked, people, objects and places will virtually collide. Reality and non-reality will blur. Students will need to understand that design is more holistic and understand how it works and functions in our lives within an increasingly physical and virtually interconnected world. They will need to address the macro and micro in our lives.

We will need to shape, critically engage with and form these future contexts. Interestingly, we will continue to see new forms of practice that will emerge, hybridising the physical and virtual. The physical will therefore be re-examined as the old informs the new and the new informs the old.

Emotional creative intelligence

As such, an 'emotional creativity' is needed where we look at design from a more integrated experience as technology converges and simultaneously diverges in our lives; designers will need to understand this and interact with the world in these changing contexts; they will need to be critically aware.

As in emotional intelligence, we will also need to have emotional creative intelligence to really, and we mean 'really', understand the problems we live in. We must respond and speculate to create future spaces. We will engage critically, playfully responding and shaping the world around us to bring new insight. We will need to apply research and share our knowledge that coexists with a focus upon quality through the marks and forms we make. Students will take a position of being the future visionaries working in a model of co-collaboration and co-creation. Students and designers will need to develop an active 'antenna' and be able to speculate and create; they will take a much more prominent position and creatively lead within broader areas of society and will become by default design curators and forecasters.

Disruptive A.I. collaborations

Disruptive collaborations will be key in order to keep those powerful interconnected computers at bay! We will collaborate with A.I. further however, as designers we will shape and purposely form disruptive collaborations with 'them'. To do this we will increasingly need to understand the need to put technology at the service of design and not design at the service of technology.

Cross-cultural flows opening up new spaces and work

Design education will further build further on 'glocal' and 'hyperlocal' relationships where we work sustainably in the local to the global. Work and people will develop cross-cultural relationships through sensitively conceived design. Educationally, we will see much further trans-cultural flows in education where the walls of institutes

become more permeable. Design value and its currency will change how we collaborate; students will be more adept at working within changing contexts. Global communications will lead to more culturally rich work within cross-cultural spaces and change thinking. Work and workspaces will be culturally re-mixed. Sustainable work and relationships will be formed that value and respect the world we live in.

The four-storey atrium of the Stirling Prize-nominated Benzie Building at Manchester School of Art, designed by Fielden Clegg Bradley, 2013.

Upside down designers

There will be a need for further critically-aware and contextually aware designers who look at the world from an upside down perspective and look at the world differently. Politics and society will need to be understood further within education environments so contextually and critically aware designers will be key. Students will be constructively critical, ask why? Have humility and empathy, be reflective, communicative, and respectful; they will have an increased contextual awareness and understanding of their role in the world.

We will continue to place emphasis on play and experimentation and this will be applied

Photo: Sebastian Mattes

The Vertical Gallery occupies the entire four-storey atrium in the Benzie Building, providing a permanent exhibition space integral to the school, which all students traverse daily to reach their studios. The work of celebrated designers such as Lucienne Day RDI (pictured), Alan Kitching RDI and Helen Storey RDI has been exhibtied each year during the annual Design Manchester festival.

certainly in the idea of industrial 'craft' where we are increasingly industrious and apply craft to enhance our lives. We will continue to test the boundaries of what is conventional and unconventional in developing new work and making the familiar unfamiliar. Design will become more inclusive, a form of total design. It will do this in understanding and acting upon who we are through our identities and communities; how and where we will live in urban and rural communities; what we do; how we travel; what we wear; what food we eat. We will consider inter-generational design in addressing health and wellbeing, sustainability in the use of materials and how we entertain ourselves.

Mind-shifters and shape-shifters 'changing our ways'

There will be a need now and in the future to promote what we call 'mind-shifters' and 'shape-shifters' where students understand and continually develop ways of 'making' but importantly allied to this are new ways of 'thinking' and new ways of 'shaping', what we call *design versatilitists*. The debate of generalist v specialist is outmoded. The design discipline will retain the 'versatile specialist' and the 'versatile generalist'. The individual nomenclature of disciplines will be questioned and we will move to the broader category of designer within undisciplinarity contexts.

A responsible academy?

Clearly, there are significant environmental issues and societal challenges. We will need to become more political and ethical in our actions in order to advocate and influence policy for the good. We will also, by understanding ethics and risk, need to push the boundaries of visual language and what is acceptable. It will become the academy's responsibility to further encourage this critical reflection and open environments. Students will develop a greater empathy, stronger humanistic understanding and understand the world through what they do. We will question making, creating, and its purpose by being more sensitive to how we use sustainable materials and build sustainable relationships and be critical practitioners understanding for what purposes and in what context.

Pedagogic designers and design constellations

As educators, we will continue to be what we call pedagogic designers. Creating environments for learning, this will be far more fluid and less institutionalised, as our everyday lives change. Design education will structurally take on less hierarchical models moving to a constellation model rather than a hierarchical one. It will change and be more adaptable with interconnected relationships and subjects. Design education will continue to step out of its own vacuum, and will engage far more broadly in the everyday. The often-cited divisions between education and industry will be increasingly positively challenged and will lead to a more interconnected space. New relationships will be formed through meaningful partnership.

Enchantment

Ultimately, what will always remain is the need for a sense of wonder and enchantment. Design will always enhance our lives and be put to meaningful purpose whether socially, economically, culturally, and politically. 'Craft' skills will be more important in our everyday lives and will play a greater part from health to politics. The ability to craft a message, to craft an object, craft a space and understand how, will need skilled crafts people. The 'craft of communication' in its broadest sense will therefore be heightened through design. Designers will help us to interact with the world to gain a deeper and more positive understanding of the world we live in.

Design education needs to create space to be enchanted, to be disruptive, to look at the world differently, making the familiar unfamiliar and to ask why. Design education is a kind of perfect imperfection. Design education needs to foster and advocate this type of space and place.

In the future Design education is and will always be this special place and design schools will need to be *a place where all things are always possible.*

…special thanks to all past, present, future students and staff who are Manchester School of Art.

Skill : A Word to Start an Argument

David Pye and Christopher Frayling
Medallists 1991 and 2003

This public dialogue on 'workmanship' and 'craftsmanship' with the craftsman in wood, teacher and writer David Pye, was mainly about the issues raised in his classic book *The Nature and Art of Workmanship* (1968). David had stressed that he saw no point in 'going through the arguments and definitions in his books all over again': he preferred to discuss matters which had arisen since *Workmanship* was first published, and since his *The Nature and Aesthetics of Design* was issued in 1978. And to take some well-aimed shots at the 'flock of duck-billed platitudes' which tended in his view to surround contemporary thinking about craftsmanship. These matters included: the aspiration of some crafts towards 'fine art', changing attitudes towards the canons of workmanship, the exhibiting of the crafts, 'tacit knowledge' and the learning of craft skills, the gospel according to St John Ruskin, the relationship between workmanship and design, and the implications for the crafts of digital technology.

FRAYLING: The first question is about developments within the crafts since *The Nature and Art of Workmanship* was published. You suggest that the crafts occupy a border ground between Fine Art and Manufacture. Since the book was published, the crafts – at least the more highly publicised examples – seem to have aspired more and more to the condition of the Fine Arts, sometimes to the neglect of traditional standards of workmanship. Could you comment on the reasons for this development and its likely effects?

PYE: Well, I think the first thing to say about that is that really these categories, Fine Art and Craft and Manufacture and so on, are fairly meaningless. I think it's an old saying that all Art is one, but no-one has ever been able to draw a line, cut-and-dried and hard-and-fast between Fine Art and Applied Art; between Fine Art and Craft; between Craft and Design – any of these things. And in this discussion I would like to say that when I say 'workman' or I suppose 'craftsman', I mean a man or a woman who simply makes things by the workmanship of risk – nothing else. I think one can quite usefully talk about a designer-craftsman, meaning a craftsman who designs what he makes, as opposed simply to a craftsman who has no hand in the design, but simply interprets somebody else's: for instance, a toolmaker, a pattern-maker. I'd also say that design is essentially an abstract and non-figurative art, and so of course is much Sculpture. And I should say, myself, that the criterion of Fine Art – the essential one – is that it is absolutely useless. It may be highly valuable, but it's quite, quite useless. That's the American Customs and Excise definition of Fine Art, and a jolly good one. It's meant for contemplation – it's not meant for use.

Well, having said that, I think that to make something which is for use imposes limits on the designer's freedom of choice – it's no good designing chairs which can't be sat on because they come to pieces, and so on. And there are far more exacting limits than that. In fact, as a matter of observation, of people working on a design, the limits on one's freedom of choice in fact help the thing and don't hinder it – why that is exactly,

I don't know. If you've got, as they say, 'a peg to hang your hat on' as a starting point, it simplifies the whole process.

And when you start producing abstract sculpture – as I've done in my time, God help me – the thing is infinitely more difficult: everything is possible, nothing can be ruled out of court. And there's something in here which keeps on saying, 'Well, that's no good, it's got to be more like this, it's got to be more like that.' And all of that is probably true, but when you have spent most of your life designing things, it really puts you into a cold sweat. So I think the fact that what they call 'the crafts' are edging rapidly, as far as I can see, in the direction of abstract art, is meaning that the process of producing them is getting much more difficult, and I think you can very, very often – regrettably often – see that. I think there's a great deal of stuff which is turned out which is terribly meretricious – it looks thin, it is thin. I think the famous saying of William Lethaby is very applicable to it – 'No art that is only one-man-deep can be very much good' – and a lot of it is, very obviously, only one-man-deep. It's highly original: well, originality – just originality and nothing else – is terribly easy to achieve. Anybody whatever can produce an original design, but, by God, what you want to do is to produce good design, and generally speaking the ingredients of good art are rather like the old Hallowe'en charm – 'something new, something old, something else…' Well, something new and something old are ingredients in any effective work of art. The point of the 'something old' is that tradition means anything but the common acceptance of it now; the one thing it doesn't mean is copying what's been done before. What it does mean is standing on the shoulders of what's been done before, starting with where what's been done before left off.

QUESTION: One thing you haven't mentioned is the price – the price that you can get for a piece of craft work – that if it's original 'you can command your own price'. If it's actually prized in a body of work which is seen nationally, it has a price which is determined by other things. And if you're young, and trying to make a name, and maybe a living, then one of the things that you're pushed towards is making a kind of art, a kind of craft which actually commands its own price and nobody else can tell you nay.

PYE: Yes, I dare say that's very true – it sounds probable – I hadn't thought of that…

FRAYLING: Another thing that lies behind the recent debate about 'craft', 'art' and 'novelty' is that in terms of your analysis of what's involved in workmanship – where there's a strong premium on what I used to call 'skill', but now tend to call 'dexterity, judgement and care' – a lot of this work is very shoddy in terms of precisely those values, although it may not be shoddy in terms of another set of values, a different kind of statement. The danger, of course, is that in the public mind the concept of 'craft' becomes associated no longer with those canons of workmanship, but with second-rate modernism. Now, that's the danger, I would have thought, from your point of view…

PYE: I think that, probably, is true.

QUESTION: One of the problems with crafts – contemporary crafts – is that many people get involved in it because it is one of the few options that they have for exploring their potential: that the fast-moving industrial framework that we have a) cannot cope with such people and is not a broad enough employer, b) is not particularly concerned with the sorts of values that we are generally concerned with – aesthetic values, taking care, doing things properly, being very good at something. So on the rebound, there is too much emphasis upon virtuoso craftsmanship for the sake of it – and for the sake of justifying the price. Actually, some of the most interesting work in the crafts seems to me to come closer to the design-making end of things.

PYE: I myself would like to see much more of people like instrument-makers for one thing, and much more of toolmakers and pattern-makers, shoemakers and all the rest of it. The workmanship of risk at its best, in fact, in any particular trade is what I would like to see.

QUESTION: If you have a high-level gallery and they put on exhibitions and you take a pine stool and you put it on top of a white plinth, the impetus to actually add a bicycle wheel on top is almost unavoidable and you actually get a Duchamp crafted object. The whole difficulty of showing design and craft in what is 'a gallery environment' by that action tends to elevate it – tends to move it in the direction of it being a work of art. Now, you take an ordinary wooden bench and put it on a plinth and you ask yourself, 'Is it Art or is it Craft?' – it becomes Art by the fact that you've put it on a plinth. A lot of things that don't look good in exhibitions would be perfectly acceptable at home. It's part of the dilemma, you see, that if you actually aspire to making things that other people would like to use, if you actually put that in an exhibition, it very often looks mundane. Because I don't ask of something I use that it should hit me in the eye every time I look at it. I don't want that out of a milk jug – I just want it to sit there docilely and contain the milk. If you put my milk jug in an exhibition, it just looks very ordinary. It doesn't have the sort of aura that an exhibition object is supposed to have.

PYE: We'd better forget the aura altogether – what I want to see is more milk jugs.

FRAYLING: There's general support for that! Let's move on now to the question of education and what is learned when you're learning a craft as distinct from what is learned when you're taught to design; a question that is stimulated by a quote from the design theorist, Philip Steadman in his recent book called *The Evolution of Design*. It goes like this: 'In the craft tradition, since there are no radical departures from the repeated type, it is possible for artefacts to be made which are technically very sophisticated, which exploit physical principles, chemical processes or the properties of materials in very subtle ways but without any of their makers having a theoretical understanding of how these effects are achieved. The principles have been discovered empirically and are embodied in the inherited design. We might speak in a sense of information being conveyed within the forms of the artefacts themselves. The craftsman knows how to make the object, he follows the traditional procedure, but in most respects he literally does not know what he is doing.'

In other words, because the craftsperson doesn't necessarily understand the physical principles of the materials he's working, and because the techniques he is using have been discovered or experienced by doing, and because he can't write the project up like a scientist writes up an experiment – because of all these things the craftsman 'does not know what he is doing'. And the question is about the two kinds of knowledge that seem to me to be implied by the quotation. We have one kind of knowledge, the formal knowledge that Philip Steadman is talking about, about the principles of materials, materials science – things that you can write down in books and learn through the transmission of hard information. And we have another kind of knowledge, the tacit knowledge that you learn by doing, of experiencing things. This quotation suggests that what the craftsman experiences isn't knowledge at all, because it doesn't look like 'bits of information'. You can't express it in those terms and therefore it doesn't count as knowledge.

So the question is: in your book on Workmanship you follow a similar observation about craftsmen not necessarily understanding the physical properties of their materials, but with a very different conclusion: 'The truth is that what we want to do is not to express the properties of materials but to express their qualities.' Could you comment on the kind of knowledge which is embodied in the qualities of workmanship…?

PYE: To call it a kind of knowledge is a bit tricky, but still, I think the essence of the answer to that question is that I contend – and I'm not by any means the only one – a designer is a problem-solver: designing is essentially a problem-solving process. It is both essentially a problem-solving process and an art; it isn't one or the other – there's no one or the other about it; it's not 'either/or', it's 'both/and'. Well now, a designer or a craftsman, or what you like qua artist, most certainly doesn't know what he's doing: no artist has ever known what he's doing, as far as I can make out. No-one has ever supposed that you can teach art – at least no-one in their right mind has ever supposed you can teach art. But you can teach artists; and that is what this place is for – it's the Royal College of Art, it isn't the Royal College of something else. And if design should be proved – how, I've no idea – to be a problem-solving activity full stop, well then, let's close this place down jolly quick.

Now, there's not the slightest reason why efficiency and art should coincide: there's not the slightest reason why making a ship, which is a very good and useful ship, should also produce a beautiful ship. The funny nonsense that was called 'functionalism' which induced me to write the first part of that book 25 years ago maintained that it did. It maintained that things looked like that because they had to look like that, and so on; whereas, as we all know, anyone who has practised design, a designer always has freedom of choice about the appearance of what he designs. And when I say 'always' I mean 'always'. I don't think I've ever come across an instance where he hadn't. I don't mean to say he has wide freedom of choice; he may have a very narrow freedom of choice, but that narrow freedom of choice may be crucial, absolutely. All that, I think, is part of the answer to this question…. One wants to remember that there is a type of mind which is afraid of the mysterious, the non-rational, the apparently inexplicable, and that of course is art. Nobody has ever said, or been able to indicate, what art is essentially. So that it's impossible to deny what this chap says – that the artist or artisan doesn't know what he's doing – but that's not really a criticism of the artist at all. What exactly can one teach when one's teaching artists? Well, the first essential of teaching art is that the teacher must be an artist himself, otherwise the whole thing is pointless. The main thing, I think, is – the main thing that can be taught, I think, is, in a sense, not teaching at all – to give the chap a chance to find out what he can really do.

QUESTION: One of the first great indictments – apart from the contemporary ones – of the Arts and Crafts Movement was in the writings of the economist, Thorstein Veblen, who said that all this stress on the roughness and on the things that were improvised was a sign of conspicuous consumption because they could then cost a lot more than everything else: if you had something which didn't look 'right' you knew that it was handcrafted and therefore was expensive, but if you had something that looked absolutely perfect it was machine-made and didn't cost so much. So it's all part of the

aristocratic conspicuous consumption syndrome – the whole ambiguity on which the
Arts and Crafts Movement is based

PYE: I should have thought that was absolute rubbish, wouldn't you? I mean, if ever there
were really high-minded people it was the early people in the Arts and Crafts Movement,
and I can't believe that they even knew what conspicuous consumption was! I mean, they
went about with their heads in the clouds, eating grass, as far as I can make out!

FRAYLING: The reason this is so relevant today is that a small group of critics – such
as Peter Fuller – is trying hard to put the 'ethics' back into 'aesthetics'. The critique of
Modernism and the Avant-garde is getting to the stage where some art critics are saying,
'Bring the ethics back and bring them back through a revised version of what John
Ruskin and William Morris were saying.'

PYE: There's another thing that might well be said before we get going on that: the thing
which Morris, more or less quoting Ruskin, said was that it was wicked to make man do
tedious, repetitive work, and that unless there was joy in the labour nothing could be
said for it. Well, some people like tedious, repetitive work; everybody, I think, likes a bit
of it now and then; and when you get to my age there isn't a hell of a lot of joy in labour,
believe me! It gets you round here! And that really is a point because, you see, in those
days people aged a lot quicker than they do now, and by the time you were forty and over
you weren't going to enjoy labour an awful lot whatever kind it was.

QUESTION: At one stage William Morris does say of the craftspeople in his workshops
that he feels a kind of guilt towards them. They were, he thinks, happy enough in their
work, but he says he is, in fact, deskilling them for work outside his workshops in the late
nineteenth century; and if he went bankrupt all his workmen, who had learned all these
skills, would be unemployable. So that was one of the reasons that he said he had to
keep going even when making a loss, because he had responsibilities towards this little
group.

PYE: That's interesting: I didn't know that.

FRAYLING: Which brings up the question about craft and design. In *The Nature and
Art of Workmanship* you define the intended design as 'an ideal form to which the
workmanship of risk may approximate'. Does this intended design need to be expressed
before craftspeople start working or can it, does it in your view, emerge from the process
of workmanship itself?

PYE: I think it certainly does want to be expressed before the chap starts working: it may
be expressed only in his head, but he's got to have a clear idea of what he's going to
do before he starts – a clear idea, but it may not be a very detailed idea. I don't think a
design ever emerges as you go on working – it evolves. I mean that the skeleton of it, the
basis of it, is there already, but when you start making, in three dimensions, something
which is only dreamed up in here or shown in a sketch on a piece of paper, or even in
a detailed drawing on a piece of paper, you see things which you hadn't allowed for
and you therefore modify the design accordingly. But you must at every stage in making
something have a clear idea of what you're trying to do, even if you keep on changing the
point of attack slightly as you go on – you must have a clear idea of why you're doing it.
And that's a very old one. The whole thing, you see, turns on the ability to visualise things

which aren't there – and that, I think, varies in different people. I believe it could be taught – I've no idea how – but I do believe it probably can be taught.

FRAYLING: In the book, you talk about 'the formalising of design' – in other words, the drawings – and the relationship between the drawings and the making of things. And you suggest these are wholly separate processes, although the latter can enhance the former – you tend to separate the two.

PYE: But the drawing is only expressing the ideal form of what's in the head, and when it's actualised by someone making from it, he's producing only an approximation to it – inevitably. But the basis of the whole thing is the thing visualised before it's drawn. That runs on to the next question, I think: can you be a good designer if you're not a good maker? Well, undoubtedly the answer is yes, you can: one has known people who could – Kaare Klint, who was perhaps the greatest furniture-designer of this century, so far anyway: I don't think ever made anything, but all the Danish designers and cabinet-makers used to say about him, 'Klint has never made anything, but we all go and ask him how to do it!' Because he knew: he knew it absolutely backwards. Moreover, although he didn't have, apparently, a very acute ability to visualise the effect of what he was designing, he did know his own limitations and he would design a piece of furniture and have a model made of it – quarter full size or one-fifth full size – put it on the mantelpiece and look at it for a year before he put it into production, so as to really make up his mind whether he'd done as much towards it as he could.

FRAYLING: It's surprising you should say that about designing and making, because there are points in your book when you imply that you can only really be a good designer if you can fully understand the possibilities of the materials you're dealing with: which seems to me to be – to take it one step further – a sort of understanding that can only emerge if you have experience of working with the material.

PYE: No, I don't believe it is; I don't think so. I don't say that people who can do the thing are common – I shouldn't think they are at all, but they do exist. Dick Russell, who was the first Professor of Furniture at the Royal College of Art, he was pretty near as good as Klint. But there is one thing to be said about it: both Klint and Dick Russell designed nearly always with the same makers, throughout their lives – Kaare Klint worked with Rudolf Rasmussen and Dick Russell with the makers at Gordon Russell Ltd. And when you work with a maker as closely as that, and you know each other as well as that, the thing becomes much more manageable. I can remember on some occasion somebody – I suppose it must have been the Rector Robin Darwin – wanted something made for the Royal College of Art by last Thursday, and I designed it on a bit of squared paper in the train coming up to London, and I chucked it at Ron Lenthall, the cabinet-maker who worked for the Furniture Department, and said: 'Look, for God's sake get on with making that, because it's wanted by last Thursday, and when you find a snag come and tell me!' And he got on with it, and then he came and said, 'Well, look, this won't work,' and so we evolved another way of doing it; and then that wouldn't work, and so we evolved another way of doing it, and put the thing together and it was a passable job. Well, that would have been absolutely impossible if one was going to a cabinet-maker whom one had never seen before or didn't know anything about. So perhaps that's a qualification that should have been made, but I'm perfectly certain that it is possible to be a very good designer and not be a maker.

FRAYLING: It would put architects in an unusual position, otherwise.

PYE: Yes, it would – it would indeed.

FRAYLING: But does your attitude to the work change if you're creating something yourself?

PYE: No, not to the work itself, no, I don't think it does. And also, of course, the other fascination of working to somebody else's design is that you learn from it. I mean, I've once or twice worked things that were designed by Professor Robert Goodden (a trained architect who became a silversmith), and he was a jolly good designer. And I started off thinking, 'I wonder what the hell he's getting at with this?' And as I went on following it I saw the point. I don't think one's attitude to the actual work – that is to say, to the process of making what's there – is any different, but the amount of tension that goes with it is quite, quite different, I think.

FRAYLING: The final question arises out of a talk that somebody gave to a group of craftspeople here a while ago, concerning numerically-controlled or digital technology. A piece of wood carving was handed round the audience, and everyone said: 'Oh, the workmanship of risk – wonderful – it breathes all the vitality of handwork.' And then the lecturer said: 'Well, actually that was the result of a computer programme, of automation; a piece of robotic technology had been programmed to reproduce that piece an infinite number of times, to copy the movements of the hand,' at which point some people in the audience then said: 'Ugh – I don't like it any more.' Now, clearly your 'proof of the pudding is in the eating' philosophy – if I can put it that way – raises this question, because the work itself couldn't tell you anything about the process because it in fact had been programmed by an extremely skilful craftsman who was able to make it reproduce the finest detail of the prototype. With variations each time. So would it worry you?

PYE: No, not a bit. The computer's only a tool like any other tool and, if it'll do that, then jolly good luck to it. No, it doesn't bother me; it's the results I want – I don't care how you get them – it doesn't matter how you get them. But I'd be fascinated to see the sort of things I make turned out by a computer – I really would – I'd love to see it. I bet I could do it better than the computer, all the same!

FRAYLING: I'd like to finish with a quotation from a D.H. Lawrence poem – one which Edward Barnsley and the Cotswold craftspeople used often to cite. In fact, Edward quoted it in his very last lecture. It's called *Things Men Have Made*. I'm sure you know it, David, and I hope you feel it is appropriate:

> Things men have made with wakened hands,
> and put soft life into
> are awake through years with transferred touch,
> and go on glowing for long years.
> And for this reason, some old things are lovely
> warm still with the life of forgotten men who made them

Education

Kenji Ekuan
Medallist 1995

Education plays an immense role in the world of the human heart and things, and their changes and mutual linking toward application to all human beings for the purpose of allowing each individual to comprehend their possession of things.

Design for everyone is design for the entire environment as well as design that is made up of all changes and mutual linking of things.

The role of education is to nurture individual people to work toward the obtaining of the entirety of this wisdom.

The world of the human heart and things – the eternal problem of education consists of applying this basic question to the entire spectrum of this wisdom.

" From early modern times education has continued to struggle with the sheer volume of knowledge."

From early modern times, up to the present, education has continued to struggle with the sheer volume of knowledge. As a result, there is said to be a tendency toward too much concentration on the material aspects of conveyance of knowledge and technological education.

When we focus upon the present problems in design education in terms of consideration of methodologies for totalising the true amalgamation of the world of things and peoples' hearts, this becomes the main subject of our inquiries. This serves as the basis of all of our courses, focusing on the hammering out of increasingly astute methodologies in our discussion sessions.

This is the major dimension of major human activities in the conveyance of education culture and the carving out of a new age. Design promotion itself has always been the essence of our efforts toward education that includes all aspects of society. Against this background, we hope to clearly delineate education as the means through which the coming age is formulated through application of good design.

Everyone is a Designer
Lessons learnt from transformative social innovation

Ezio Manzini
Medallist 2012

We are already living in transition phase: the 21st Century sees all of us catapulted into a risky, turbulent and complex reality that can be understood as a mesh of long lasting crises (the crisis of all the 20th Century social, cultural and economic models) and/or as a broad contradictory transition towards a new form of society. Hopefully, a sustainable one.

In this framework, contemporary society is a huge future-building laboratory where everything that belonged to the mainstream way of thinking and doing in the 20th Century is changing and will change: from everyday life and the very idea of wellbeing, to the large socio-technical eco-systems in which they exist. This is, a learning process of which design is part and in which it could and should play a major role.

Given that, what skill set should design experts have to play this role? To answer this question two steps must be done: [1] To recognise the emerging design features (to recognise the on-going changes in design culture and practice and the emerging skills that, in the crisis of the 20th century models, characterise it). [2] To understand the needed specific culture and practices (the ones permitting emerging design to become an agent of change towards a resilient and sustainable society).[1]

Emerging design features. Today, the basic features of emerging design are already clear. And they are very different from those dominant in the 20th Century. The main one is that its focus has shifted from "objects" (meaning products, services and systems) towards "ways of thinking and doing" (meaning methods, tools, approaches and, as we will see, design cultures). In so doing, design becomes an agent capable of tackling widely differing issues adopting a human-centered approach: from traditional product-oriented design processes to complex and often intractable social, environmental and even political problems). A second main change, linked to the first, is that all design processes are, de facto, to be considered co-design activities involving a variety of actors: professional designers, other kinds of experts and final users.

Given that, as anticipated, a second step has to be taken. In fact, the basic features of emerging design and the resulting capabilities of design experts, don't, per se, indicate which kind of change they will be used for. In short, emerging design could be, and indeed already is, a driver of change for very different directions. That is, towards both, sustainable or unsustainable societies. The question therefore becomes: what are the practices and the culture needed to make of emerging design a potential driver in the right direction?

New design practices. Emerging design (for sustainability) is an activity that promotes and supports contradictory, open-ended processes in which different stakeholders bring their specific skills and their culture. This co-design process the design experts are part

---

[1] These notes are largely based on: Ezio Manzini, *Design, When Everybody Designs. An Introduction to Design for Social Innovation* (Cambridge, Mass: MIT Press 2015)

of can be seen as a social conversation in which everybody is allowed to bring ideas and take action, even though these ideas and actions could, at times, generate problems and tensions. In short, this means that these involved actors are willing and able to establish a dialogic cooperation. That is, a conversation in which listening is as important as speaking. [2]

The complex and dynamic nature of these co-design processes is what gives emerging design the possibility of operating as a real agent of change towards better ways of living and producing. In short, they can be grouped in two main modalities: [1] Design with communities, when design experts collaborate with active groups of people in making a given solution more accessible and more capable of lasting in time. [2] Design for favourable eco-systems, when design experts conceive and develop material and immaterial artefacts capable of making a whole eco-system more favourable for new initiatives to emerge, flourish, spread and connect.

A new design culture. Emerging design (for sustainability) should participate to these broad co-design processes feeding them with ideas, visions, and proposals. That is, supporting design actions with visions of sustainable futures. This emerging design feature is, in my view, a main pillar of what should be the 21st Century design culture. Where this should design culture come from? A full, well-reasoned answer to this question is beyond the scope of these notes. However, here I can summarise some points that seem to me particularly relevant.

This new design culture has not to be invented from zero, but can be built interacting with the growing wave of transformative social innovation [3] and with the new set of interlinked scenarios it is generating and partially enhancing. [1] The scenario of distributed systems, intended as the infrastructure of a resilient society. [2] The scenario of social economy, intended as an ecology of different economies. [3] The scenario of relational qualities, intended as the quality to be searched for regenerating social commons and proposing an idea of wellbeing based on them. [4] And, finally, [4] the scenario of cosmopolitan localism, intended as the condition in which locality and connectedness, identity and diversity live together, giving richness to experience and resilience to the whole society. [5]

---

[2] Richard Sennet, *Together. The Rituals, Pleasures and Politics of Cooperation* (New Haven and London: Yale University Press 2012); Carl DiSalvo, *Adversarial Design* (Cambridge, Mass: MIT Press 2012) ; Erling Björgvinsson, Pelle Ehn & Per-Anders Hillgren, "Agonistic participatory design: working with marginalised social movements", *CoDesign: International Journal of CoCreation in Design and the Arts*, 8:2-3 (2012), 127-144

[3] Transformative social innovation is a subset of social innovation as a whole. Indeed, there are innovations that go in different directions from the one I am indicating: ones which are not radical in character, but limit themselves to proposing incremental modifications, or which go in a direction that is completely opposite to that of environmental and social sustainability. The expression, 'transformative social innovation', was introduced in the ambits of the European research project, Transit, which ended in 2017. The task was to investigate 'transformative social network initiatives and networks in an attempt to understand the process of societal transformation' in Transit, *Doing Things Differently*. Transit Brief #1, 2017) *http://www.transitsocialinnovation.eu*

[4] Ezio Manzini, Virginia, Tassinari, *Sustainable qualities: powerful drivers of social change*, in Crocker. R. Lehmann, S. (edited by), *Motivating Change*, London: Earthscan, 2013; Ezio Manzini, *Making Things Happen: Social Innovation and Design*, in Design Issue, Vol 30, Number 1, Winter 2014.

[5] Ezio Manzini, *Politics of the Everyday* (London: Bloomsbury, to be published in February 2019)

The Future

Industrial Design : Art or Science?

Sir Misha Black

*Written for the American Society of Interior Designers' (ASID) Bulletin,
Philadelphia, January 1965*

Art and design are somewhere linked. We know that we, as industrial designers, are
not only engineers concerned with man-machine relationships, not only ergonomists,
marketing experts and the rest of our public relations image. We really care about what
the products we design look like and feel like, and how well they serve the community.
We glow with modest pride if one of our designs is acclaimed by other designers
as being of outstanding quality. Sales alone (while primary to our very existence as
designers) are not the only criteria by which we measure our success or failure. We
retain secret standards for our judgement of design merit which sometimes give us
momentary pleasure and more often prolonged anguish.

Man does not live by bread alone, nor do industrial designers judge their work only by
the standards of their clients' sales graphs and dividends. This is part of the process
which entitles us to be accepted as a profession and not a trade. We cling, if rather
desperately at times, to some ultimate standards. Firstly, our work must be socially useful
and, secondly, it must have a quality which transcends its practical use. The social value
of industrial design has often been evaluated, more often to its credit than otherwise.

That overt value I do not need to emphasise except to say, in passing, that I do not
believe that only what personally pleases me is good design and all else bad, or that only
products which have been bleached of all colour, decoration, enrichment and frivolity
are 'good', and that all else must be eschewed by the conscientious designer as though
it were dross. I see no moral turpitude in an electric cooker being embellished or an
automobile so enriched that it makes their owners feel nine feet tall, so long as it has not
been made unreasonably expensive or dangerous. Its social function is to give pleasure
as well as efficient service. But Palladio summarised all this in the sixteenth century:
'Although variety and things new may please everyone, yet they ought not to be done
contrary to the precepts of art and contrary to that which reason dictates.'

Some years ago Walter Dorwin Teague, who has said some very wise things
about industrial design, explained that there are four design objectives – efficiency,
convenience, economy and simplicity, but he then added the fifth ingredient of 'beauty'
which, he said, 'the designer contributes out of his inner resources'.

'This kind of beauty we are called on to create must,' he continued, 'be an outward
and visual interpretation of the inner values of the object designed.' With that I whole-
heartedly agree, as do most others who have theorised about industrial design, but is
that visual expression of the inner values of the object ART or is it something else?

Let me declare my position without prevarication. I do not believe that industrial design
has anything to do with ART, if by ART we mean the rare quality which has enabled
men to build the Acropolis, paint the ceiling of the Sistine Chapel, compose the Fifth
Symphony or write *Macbeth*. We could not, in all humility, begin to compare even the
most distinguished practitioners of our profession with Michelangelo, Rembrandt,
Shakespeare, Beethoven or Cezanne.

This is not a question of scale, time or opportunity. We do not clarify the situation by taking the point of view of the ant who, when asked by an elephant why he was so small, answered with justified irritability: 'Of course I'm small I've been very ill and lost a lot of weight.'

I feel allowed to make these doubt-engendering comparisons between pygmies and giants because I, myself, am a pygmy designer and have battled with the desire to justify my own work by asserting that it is at least of the same order as other works of art, even if minor in quality. Philosophers from Plato onwards have propped my self-esteem by equating at least one aspect of art with formal mathematical qualities which Plato described as '...straight lines and circles, and the plane or solid figures which are formed out of them by turning lathes and rulers and measures of angles; for these I affirm to be not only relatively beautiful, like other things, but they are externally and absolutely beautiful'.

It is conceivable that Plato may, in theory, be right, but certainly no typewriter, automobile, prefabricated building, kitchen stove or machine tool has possessed that elusive quality which characterises the fine arts.

Art, I believe, is the 'expression of emotion' or, as put slightly differently by the American philosopher Suzanne Langer, 'art is the creation of forms symbolic of human feeling'. Art is concerned with the epitomising of the emotional life of a whole society at a moment in its history; a great work of art makes the spectator or listener or reader conscious of what Mondrian has called 'the union of the individual with the universe'.

It is conceivable that an artist might use the solid geometry propounded by Plato as a means for the expression of his emotion, as a medium through which he unconsciously expresses and crystallises the religious experience of a society, but this has little to do with the problem of improving the operation of a heavy-duty machine tool, producing an elegant body for an automobile, or designing a corporate image for an industrial undertaking.

It is theoretically feasible that an industrial designer might produce a minor work of art as he undertakes his more prosaic tasks, but if he were to do so (and personally I doubt whether that is ever, in fact, possible) that would be an accidental coincidence, and the emotional quality of the product would be quite separate from its usefulness.

So I suggest we jettison all pretensions to being artists – at least those of us who have any. (As Ernest Hemingway was advised by a critic to 'take these false hairs off your chest, Mr Hemingway', so we could say to ourselves '...take that long hair out of your eyes, Mr Designer'.)

Creativity

But if industrial design is not ART, what is there about it which gives us stomach ulcers, which drives us towards an image of perfection, which sends our families and staff round the bend as we strive for design solutions which neither the fee we receive nor the standards our clients set demand.

The answer, I submit, is that we have smelt the sweet, intoxicating, heady, habit-forming, irresistible aroma of creativity. We have found that, within the boundaries of doing efficiently and ably the jobs set to us, there lies the possibility of creative achievement.

There can be no art without creativity, but creativity is not synonymous with art. Creativity is simply the making of something, or finding a method of performing a task, in a new way which does not exactly repeat what has previously been done. Creativity is childbirth, it is cooking a meal with originality, it is finding a new way to spin a cricket ball, it is making a man fly, and it is industrial design. To create is to approach the vision of God: once the capacity to create has been experienced, all other activity becomes of secondary importance.

Creativity germinates tranquillity. A design taken to its final three-dimensional form can, for a moment, provide the same sense of quietude as others find by solving mathematical problems. I say momentary because the tranquillity is, for the designer, only a pause before he is racked by doubts as to the validity of his creation, conscious of its failings. He is immediately spurred by its (for him) partial success to tackle the next job with the ever-receding hope that one day he may produce something with which he is completely satisfied for longer than the moment of its materialisation.

In this generation of uneasy conscience, the moments of creativity provide the moments of self-justification, the sense of having inscribed oneself in history, faint though the signature may be. To create, or to participate in the creation of a new design, is to ensure a pale immortality. It is more satisfying than carving one's name on an ancient monument or scribbling on a wall. But if our work allows us, infrequently, that special, rare pleasure of creative accomplishment, it also brings special obligations. We must pay for our moments of euphoria by the gravity of social responsibility.

You will not want me to restate in lugubrious detail the problem of the designer in meeting the demands of markets peopled by those with tastes which differ from his own. This has been so often discussed as almost to have become a design conference theme song, awaiting only equally anxious and conscious composers to put the words to music.

But recently I read a description of this problem which was so clear and succinct as to make it impossible for me to resist quoting it. It comes from *The Principles of Art* by R. G. Collingwood.

'In so far as the artist feels himself at one with his audience, this will involve no condescension on his part; it will mean that he takes it as his business to express not his own private emotions, irrespectively of whether any one else feels them or not, but the emotions he shares with his audience. Instead of conceiving himself as a mystagogue, leading his audience as far as it can follow along the dark and difficult paths of his own mind, he will conceive himself as his audience's spokesman, saying for it the things it wants to say but cannot say unaided. Instead of setting up for the great man who imposes upon the world the task of understanding him, he will be a humbler person, imposing upon himself the task of understanding his world, and thus enabling it to understand itself'.

Collingwood was writing about ART, and I am not sure that I would unquestioningly accept his view in relation to that major activity, but I believe it is apposite to our job of industrial design. In the final analysis we are producing things for people and not only for our own self-satisfaction or the applause of a small group of cognoscenti. Collingwood's use of the word 'mystagogue' inevitably leads me to design methodology. Is methodology mystagogic or has it some real value in improving our work, reducing our anguish and increasing our value to society?

It is understandable that designers should search for an academic base to give support to their seemingly effervescent occupation. So to methodology have been added ergonomics, cybernetics, motivational and marketing research, symbolic logic, psychology, decision theory, closed-loop control theory, project planning, dynamic anthropometry, information retrieval, old uncle computer and all.

I have no quarrel with these worthy and often essential pursuits. (Envy and admiration of those who really understand and can operate these techniques dominate all my other reactions.) But I must raise two mild objections to the overenthusiastic cyberneticists and the overeager ergonomists. Firstly these sophisticated techniques are too often applied to minor design problems which ordinary common sense and experience could more easily and rapidly solve. (Computer hammers to crack thin-shelled industrial design problem nuts) Secondly these techniques for research and logical analysis are not the direct concern of the industrial designer.

New unity

Before I am torn to pieces by my colleagues at the Royal College of Art and banned from Ulm, let me explain more precisely what I mean. I appreciate the value of analysis and research (I don't mind if designers analyse their pencils before they start to use them) so long as the research and analysis is completely honest and, in its scope and depth, is reasonably related to the project in hand. But investigation, research and analysis can be done by investigators, researchers and analysers – it does not need to be done by industrial designers, nor are the people who do it performing the activity of industrial design.

The job of designers is to take the result of the research and analysis, sift the verbiage from the kernel of truth and then use the facts which remain as a springboard for their creative design decisions. Importance as a designer depends on the ability to spring forward, to find new solutions, to create new forms, to create new unity, to produce something which has never before existed in the exact form of its new creation.

There is no reason why industrial designers should not ergonomise or cybernate or research or analyse, but while they do so they are ergonomists or cyberneticists or researchers doing jobs which others specialised in those disciplines could do as well. The only advantage in the industrial designer's personally undertaking these research tasks is that they may provide the period of gestation necessary for all creative activity.

I have always been guided by the slogan which I read of thirty-five years ago in an early efficiency magazine: 'Never do anything yourself which someone else can do equally well', and that releases me personally from almost all research. But this does not imply that the industrial designer is a nice artistic chap who waits until others have done the research and analysis and then produces a new or improved solution as though he were gilding a lily or sugarcoating a pill. Firstly, the industrial designer must be able to evaluate the research and analysis, and that requires experience in these fields. Secondly, the industrial designer is firmly anchored to the ground by the constraints of the manufacturing processes and the materials from which the product is made. Unless he understands the whole sequence which translates raw materials into finished products or services, he must be content to be the butterfly hovering uneasily around industry instead of being an integrated participant within the industrial complex. (An industrial designer without engineering training or experience is like a cook who has never been taught how to thicken a sauce or make pastry – it makes the job unnecessarily difficult.)

The industrial processes are the matrix for the designer's creativity. To be conscious of human needs but unable to translate them into workshop drawings is useful for those who direct and manage design, but useless for those who, themselves, wish to design; those who must transform the blank sheet of paper into a blueprint for production. I have allowed myself the doubtful pleasure of demolishing my own pretensions. But I would not have you feel that I doubt in any way the importance of our profession or its immense potentiality. I believe that eventually the industrial designer can fill a role in the engineering and other producer industries comparable to that of the architect in the building industry.

I doubt whether the aesthetic content of mass-produced objects can ever be of great strength, and one must find some compensation in the million repetition of objects (each with the capacity for giving minor visual and tactile pleasure) for the intensity of a single major work of art in which the emotional life of a whole society is synthesised. Be that as it may, the industrial designer, given a further decade of education, experience and opportunity, could become the vehicle for the expression of the social function of industry, concerned with all visual aspects of industrial production, from the product itself to the environment in which it is produced and distributed. Ultimately he may become the new kind of artists which Herbert Read has described in *Icon and Idea*.

The future scale of the artist is not domestic, nor even monumental, but environmental: the artist of the future will not be a painter or a sculptor or an architect, but a new moulder of plastic forms who will be painter and sculptor and architect in one – not an adulterous mixture of all these talents, but a new kind of talent that subsumes and supersedes them all.

Those are heroic words, and it is difficult to imagine more than a handful of people individually meeting that noble specification. But the need exists for the co-ordinator of many talents into the unified team which could well be the 'moulder of plastic forms', and this co-ordinator it is conceivable that the industrial designer may eventually become. As the architect coordinates his consultants and executants in the building industries, so could the industrial designer eventually serve the engineering industries.

This is a counsel of perfection, but it is useful to retain a vision of the horizon while occupied with more immediately practical ends. There is no harm in the designer's visualising himself eventually as a man of social responsibility and personal authority if he can simultaneously remain sufficiently humble to concentrate all his energies and capacities on the design of an electric toaster.

Industrial design is not art, but nor is it only science and technology. It is a creative process in which engineering necessity is equated with human needs. It is a new profession in its own right in which I for one am proud to be enrolled.

Fitness For What Purpose?

Sir Misha Black

Written August 1974, for Design Magazine

In the May 1935 issue of *Design for Today* the full-page illustration facing the leading article was a photograph of a building wreathed in scaffolding. It was captioned: 'THE MODERN SPIRIT: removing Victorian decoration from an office building in London.' No further editorial comment was needed to ensure that this spirit merited acclaim. The magazine was published by the Design and Industries Association, and the May issue celebrated its first 25 years of activity.

Designers and their aficionados in the 1930s were not troubled by doubt. They proudly continued a century of tradition from William Morris to Lethaby, supported by the theory and practice of those who were certain that 'good design' could be identified and that it was morally desirable.

'The Modern Spirit' in 1975 (When the DIA celebrated its Diamond Jubilee) was less clearly delineated. The social and resources problems which must be resolved on a world scale are now more generally comprehended; their magnitude dwarfs concern with the minutiae of comparing one cup and saucer with another for aesthetic commendation; lack of confidence in the abilities of our architects and designers has made the old more palatable than the new, conservation more acceptable than innovation.

The DIA now concerns itself more with materials and energy resources than with the form and decoration of artefacts; aesthetics have been deposed by social responsibility; its old slogan 'Fitness for Purpose' was replaced, at a recent conference, by 'Fitness for Need'. The majority of students of industrial design choose these projects which are socially desirable, which serve world needs, as they visualise them, rather than encourage the proliferation of consumer products. The Design Council balances its responsibility for consumer products by its involvement in engineering design *per se*.

I need not elaborate on this swing from what is desired to what is necessary; most people of good will now pay at least lip service to social obligation even if this does not perceptibly alter their own life style. The Royal College of Art in association with the Design Council, the Royal Society of Arts, the Society of Industrial Artists and Designers and the Design and Industries Association organised a major international seminar and exhibition in the spring of 1976 to demonstrate the activities of designers within the matrix of social responsibility. It was an impressive display of what has been achieved and a platform for planning a more direct and beneficial involvement of industrial designers in meeting the needs of the majority of the world's population whose poverty and hunger shame the profligate minority.

Amidst the thunder of what Victor Papanek has called 'the new revisionism' in design, one might well question whether any justification remains in the design function as it was visualised even 10 years ago, whether there is a need for quality when quantity is so obvious a requirement, whether it matters what a bus or an electric kettle look like so long as they operate efficiently.

The quality of design

Perhaps this is no place for a discourse on aesthetics, but I ask you to accept that art is an essential element in the structure of all civilisations, be they primitive, sophisticated or decadent; any attempt to write the history of mankind which eliminated reference to music, drama, dancing, literature, architecture and craftwork would be a travesty. Art is an essential manifestation of the human spirit which succumbs only to abject poverty. If it can be argued, therefore, that design is even partially an art, then it also has a function which is not wholly determined by material needs. I believe this to be so.

"Industrially produced objects can have the elegance of a mathematical equation."

I do not claim that industrial design, even when undertaken with absolute dedication, is an art of the same order as music or painting; to compare a bicycle with the Michelangelo 'Pietà' or kitchen utensils with a Sung bowl would obviously be ludicrous, but industrially produced objects can have the elegance of a mathematical equation, a quality of exactly suiting their purpose, so that they are tuned to the emotional and practical needs of a society at a moment in its history. They fall within Alberti's definition of beauty as 'the harmony and concord of all the parts achieved in such a manner that nothing could be added or taken away or altered except for the worse'.

The relationship of form and function has been endlessly debated, so may I ask you only to concede that there is a casual relationship between art and industrial design even if design for mass production is a partial art, lacking the essential ingredient of humanity. Nevertheless, in the use and contemplation of an industrial product, it is possible to sense the skill and sensitivity of its designer and by empathy experience the pleasure and excitement of his creativity. We have all taken pleasure in the objects we have owned and used; this is a modest and innocuous satisfaction, so what reason is there for the present violent reaction against design as though the very qualities for which we previously praised it have become reasons for condemnation?

The source of this antagonism springs from the late 1920s. Until then all design theory and proselytisation ran in a direct line from William Morris, through the arts and crafts movement to the Bauhaus. Designers were missionaries for a new world in which beauty would conquer ugliness and in doing so produce an environment in which social justice could more easily be ensured. Around 1929, however, a new breed of designers appeared on stage: they were Americans, their scenario was the relationship of design to profit. They coined the phrase 'industrial design' and proved that design could be used as an effective marketing weapon.

The relationship of design to salesmanship was not a new concept; it was a factor in the Great Exhibition of 1851; it was the need to make Britain self-sufficient without 'enemy products' which ensured Board of Trade support for the embryonic DIA in

1915. But it was not until Raymond Loewy, Walter Dorwin Teague, Henry Dreyfus and Norman bel Geddes demonstrated that design could, in some situations, be the crucial factor in achieving sales, that the streams divided and have since progressed in uneasy parallelism. If 'good design is good business', as the Council of Industrial Design was eager to claim in the 1950s, then it could be argued conversely that what is good for business is 'good design'. It is down this slope that the ethics of design have slid to enable industry to claim that profitability is the only standard for judging excellence in design.

It is not for me to question the morality of competitive trading, but it is justifiable for designers to question whether their skill and experience are most usefully engaged in creating demand for products and services which serve no purpose except to satisfy the desire for novelty and personal acquisition. While industrial design was a young and struggling profession such considerations were submerged by the need to find jobs to do and clients who believed that designers had any part to play in industrial enterprise, benign or nefarious as it may have been. Now that the profession has achieved a degree of authority its new entrants survey its prospects with a more sceptical eye.

The new practitioners have two alternatives; they can either decide only to work on projects which are, as they see it, morally justified, or accept commissions which they believe to be morally reprehensible, give their clients and their customers what they believe they will buy and jettison any pretensions to keeping alive even a faint pulse of artistic conviction. Neither alternative is satisfactory; the former leaves the field clear for the second-class, meretricious designer to determine the form of the majority of industrial production, the latter complacently panders to the lowest common denominators of human behaviour. This willing renunciation of creative responsibility is heralded by some critics as a new art form: 'camp' is permissible fun, Los Angeles the epitome of civilised living, graffiti is submitted to aesthetic analysis, students with intense seriousness and expert craftsmanship spend months fixing a zip fastener to a cup and saucer or printing a book on slices of synthetic brown bread.

'But being comical', as Stevie Smith wrote, 'does not ameliorate the misery.' It is only when no positive stance seems feasible that opting out with a merry laugh becomes the only tolerable action.

Return to first base

We cannot afford to squander our civilisation, imperfect though it be, by turning from it with puritanical self-righteousness or by wearing a clown's disguise. A way must be found to justify our own work as designers and to signpost a route for the students as they cautiously examine our progress. We must reaffirm that the aesthetic component in design justifies our dedication to this activity and yet, believing this, renounce any conscious aesthetic attitude.

The formal qualities of the objects which produce our man-made environment, be they as small as a chair or possessing the grandeur of a bridge, must arise from an absolute devotion to the proposition that form and function are a unity. We could usefully again unfurl the ancient DIA banner and proclaim 'Fitness for Purpose' as our prime motivator. Our society is in turmoil as we uneasily begin to appreciate the technological and social implications of the electronic revolution as instant communication makes us conscious of world-wide involvement and responsibility while being unable to guarantee even the bare essentials of life to the majority of the people of the 'global village'.

Against this background, any aesthetic which consciously celebrates our society is impossible, at least for designers who must produce products or systems for immediate consumption. We should, therefore, to the extent that it is possible, renounce formal preconception. We should approach each new problem from the base of practicality – how can it most economically be made, how will it function most effectively, how can maintenance be simplified, how can the use of scarce materials be minimised?

An absolute concern with practicalities will produce new formal solutions as technology constantly develops: when alternatives present themselves during the design process, the aesthetic sensitivity of the designer will determine his selective decision, but this should remain a searching process and not be seen as the opportunity for imposing a preconception of formal appropriateness. The difference between an arrogant conscious aesthetic and a conscientious searching for the most elegant solution is fundamental to my argument. During a period in which we can move in 30 years from detesting Victorian architecture to conserving it, it is not surprising that a conscious aesthetic applied to the useful arts results more often in styling than in style.

Designers who adopt this attitude, who believe, as I do, that our concern is with the elegant solution to practical problems without posturing or histrionics, can now find an adequate market for their knowledge and experience. Buyers, be they engineers, bulk purchasers or housewives, are now more ready than they were a decade ago to accept that practicality and simplicity are more essential attributes than flamboyance. I suspect that at least a proportion of the products and systems which disgrace our industries are the way they are because sales managers misjudge their markets and because their designers are sometimes incompetent. It is significant that the Mark 2 Capri has jettisoned the fake ventilators which embellished the earlier model and that the Design Centre has become a national institution.

I know that design which is distinguished by absolute honesty and which is free of pretension remains the exception and not the rule, but opportunities now exist for those designers who are prepared only to undertake work which does not negate their professional integrity. As I believe this to be true, I have been prepared to accept some responsibility for educating a new generation of industrial designers.

Decoration, fantasy and symbolism

What I have so far written applies more to kitchen appliances and telephones, trains and machine tools, bathroom fittings and hospital equipment, than to china and glass, clothes and wallpaper. The desire to decorate is an endemic human characteristic. However, too often, alas, it is a trivial disturbance to an otherwise agreeable plain surface.

But surface enrichment we must often have, and even if our generation lacks a generally accepted language of decoration which supplies the pattern-makers with a base for improvisation, there is satisfaction in the transient quality of decoration, in the swift swings of fashion which ephemera provides without undue extravagance or profligacy.

Man dreams as well as eats and is not satisfied by practicality alone. Even if we in the

Western world should ever accept egalitarian austerity, there would still be a need for fun and for fantasy, for theatres and fair grounds as well as schools and hospitals. There is a need for vulgarity as well as elegance, for gaiety as well as seriousness.

To meet these unquantifiable needs, designers are needed with a different approach from the one which I have so far annunciated. Those with the requisite attitudes and talents too often now work, however, only for a small coterie, laughing at their own private jokes. For a short time in Britain the art school ebullience exploded into the High Street. Skirts leaped high up thighs, Carnaby street became a symbol for a release from parental respectability. This image is already tired and tarnished and needs replacement by a new wave of equal transience.

The designers who are motivated by irrationality are more closely allied to the fine arts than to industrial design. Their invention is at the outer fringe of art, but they celebrate the unpredictability of man, the instincts which make people climb mountains and make love. But they share one characteristic with the designers of useful three-dimensional objects. This is technical knowledge and skill. Many years of learning and practice are necessary before any designer is able to practise with professional competence, and this he or she must have whether they decide to dedicate their skills and creativity to design for intermediate technology or urban transportation, to book design or fashion fabrics. The British colleges of art and design have now accepted that professionalism postulates proficiency. Skilled designers now exist in good measure (which was not so when the DIA was formed); they must now decide how to apply their knowledge and abilities.

In our present epoch of social and technological upheaval no industrial designer can have the absolute conviction which justifies flamboyant expressionism. We should, instead, approach our tasks with humility and accept that we are usually more usefully engaged in making minor improvement to existing products and systems than in radical innovation. The practice of industrial design requires exacting standards of technical proficiency and dedication to the search for elegant solutions to practical problems. 'Fitness for Purpose' is as appropriate a slogan today as it was half a century ago, but we must now evaluate the purpose before deciding whether it justifies the search for a solution which will fit it: an elegant bomb is still a bomb.

"An elegant bomb is still a bomb."

Industrial design is not an isolated activity; it is linked to engineering, to the crafts, to decoration and, tenuously, to the fine arts. It is an element in the total activity which produces the man-made environment and thus justifies both approbation and anxiety. In Danish GOD DESIGN means good design. We should rigorously examine the feet of this god for traces of clay, but repair rather than topple its essential edifice.

The Other 99%

Lorraine Gamman
Award 2006

'Our designs probably give meaning to only 1% of the world's population; so we need to start designing for the 99% if we want to have an influence on the future' suggested the CEO of the Danish Design Centre (Juul-Sørensen, 2014). Yet in the last forty years of the neo-liberal period, mainstream design in the West is not designing for the 99%; instead it is (or has been) the handmaiden of capitalism creating designs for those who can afford them and profits for the already rich.

Design history reminds us that in the UK, between the Great Exhibition (1851) and the Festival of Britain (1951), design emerged alongside industrial production with at least some social democratic focus in its ambition to problem solve. But, in the post-war years, design's 'problem solving' focus has been overshadowed by its capacity to add value to products, experiences, services and spaces to deliver desire and differentiation in relationship to the market. Consequently, the dominant account of the 'consumer' (rather than 'user' or social 'need') has heavily influenced design. The brand heroes of contemporary capitalism, including Apple, appear to design for planned obsolescence and whilst they are innovative and address social communication, they are all about profit.

Guy Julier (2017) has eloquently discussed how design, during the last 40 years, has assumed a more central role in actively shaping and reinforcing, our current economic systems. More importantly, design's ability to shape our personal and social understandings and connect them to the market has made it a force to be reckoned with.

Yet alongside market-led design there remain, on the margins, heroic social design narratives that continue to be heard, that use design in different ways to design different 'things' (Björgvinsson et al., 2012). Our design schools are full of the voices and outputs of young designers who idealistically try to use social and sustainable design to find new ways to improve the world, to design for more than profit and to take a 'social responsive' (Gamman & Thorpe, 2006; 2011) or 'activist' (Julier, 2013) stance. This work often remains on the fringes of what is known as 'design'. Yet "we are currently witnessing a 'social design' moment", according Armstrong et al. (2014) in a report for the Arts and Humanities Research Council. This report suggests that social designers are those who 'make change happen towards collective and social ends, rather than predominantly commercial objectives.'

There is very little data available on what proportion of UK design and design education is engaging with social design challenges. This lack of measurement is of concern if we are to continue to make the case for design addressing social issues, which involves radically transforming how we teach. As Thackara (2006) put it, as designers evolve 'from being the individual authors of objects or buildings, to be facilitators of change among large groups of people, the way we teach design has to change' (and has done so). But a lot more upskilling of design educators is needed (not just on sustainability but also social design best practice). If we wish to steer ALL design projects run in design school towards equating with UN Sustainable and Development Goals, as some schools in Denmark appear to be considering in order to save the planet, we need to up our game (see Centre for Co Design Research at Royal Danish Academy of Fine Arts whose approaches are being incorporated by many other design courses located at KADK).

The international Beazley Design Awards 2017 were a revelation in that they finally recognised not only social design and design activism, but also the way some of these projects were resourced i.e. from crowdfunding and other enterprising approaches. If we are to make the UN's goals for sustainability more influential in design schools and ultimately realise them, we need to share more information about how social design can happen. Also, what new economic models exist. We need to better understand the ways in which design can be social in its means as well as its ends. As Manzini (2009) has pointed out, we need to better understand 'designers as connectors and facilitators, as quality producers, as visualisers and visionaries, as future builders (or co-producers). Designers as promoters of new business models. Designers as catalysers of change.' Yet design education's reliance on engagement with industry, business and enterprise funding ensures its proximity to the market (even our UK students have to pay fees, make a profit and be understood as consumers) means that future roles and pathways are not always distinct from the old ones. Worse, the Higher Education Funding Council for England (HEFCE) (2018) indicates that whilst 30,000 students took design courses in 2012–13 and 2015–16, 'only a quarter of them end up in the top three jobs associated with design' and that this does not compare well with other vocational courses such as teacher training, nursing, medicine, dentistry and architecture (Dawood, 2018). All the more reason for better understanding and finding ways to measure the slowly changing roles of designers who work both for the market but also engage with local communities. Whilst participatory design techniques can help us understand the future better from the point of view of collective need, often such approaches are invisible or have a relation back to the market that is not understood. Even if social design, defined by Chen et al. (2016), appears to engage with different economic models to facilitate this as explained below, deriving from social design social innovation and social entrepreneurship, how this is delivered can be unclear and entangled so more upskilling for design educators is needed in order to recognise and be precise about our social design teaching and learning aims. Some of these methods and understandings are still very new and need to be 'unpacked', as Thomas Markussen (2017) points out. His article lists the different qualities of social approaches, as can be seen in Table 1 (on the next page).

To take social design forward, the Design Against Crime Research Centre has created many socially engaged projects working with local communities in Camden (*publiccollaborationlab.com*), as well as those in prison (*makeright.org*) and they have taught us a lot about what it might be like when everybody designs (Manzini, 2015). We see the potential for using design and entrepreneurship models in new ways, but we also recognise that if the 'social' turn of our design focus is to make a difference it needs to be substantiated by clear evidence as to why it is important/works, and transparent about the economic arrangements involved. This means subjecting untested design case studies to more evidence-based measurement of social impact, as we are now doing; addressing NESTA's (Mulgan, 2014) observation that social design 'has had little external measurement and evaluation', we are busy gathering, as best we can, statistical evidence about the value of the new design models we promote.

And so, the future of design is contested and uncertain and with it the future of design education. In such a scenario, the focus of design to understand the present so as to shape the future, to move from what is to what could be (or should be), should be

Table 1. Markussen (2017) Social Design Framework.

Summarises the analysis of research literature presented in this article

	Social Innovation	Social entrepreneurship	Social design
Aim	To remedy system errors in order to improve living standards, welfare service provision, sustainable consumption and delivery.	To identify market errors as opportunities for bringing abut a new social equilibrium for a needy group in society.	To improve life conditions for a disadvantaged and confined social group or community.
Modus operandi	Participatory processes based on cross-sectorial systematic approach to foster social change.	Participatory processes based on a business approach to foster social change.	Co-design processes and material aesthetic practices take centre stage in the form of infra-structuring contradictory interests and resources.
Social values	Social value is conceived of in broad terms as 'the common good' and must to the benefit of large segments or 'social movements' in society.	Social value is tightly coupled with a concern also to perform financially.	Social value is conceived of as a small, but decisive qualitative change in the form of a re-distribution of identities or interpersonal relationships.
Locus of innovation	The innovation is created out of interactive processes shaped by the collective sharing of knowledge between a wide range of organisations, sectors and civic society.	The innovation is created by either 'the lone visionary' entrepreneur or the social enterprise.	Social design is created out of a collaborative design process where designers involve a specific group of citizens, public and private partners to achieve social change.
Effect	Large-scale transformations that lead to a new social equilibrium and that allow others to copy ideas and transfer the innovation.	Large-scale transformations that lead to a new social equilibrium and that allow others to copy ideas and transfer the innovation.	Micro-scale effects that may reach a mesa-level, but these effects rarely 'break out of their limited frame'.
Project examples	Samatarian Mobile Care Complex.	Place de Bleue MYC4 The Liter of Light project Basaglia's Democratic Psychiatry Logik & Co.	Social Games against Crime.

applied and clearly addressed by all those involved in design education. This work should not be managed by a cabal of design gatekeepers or their benefactors/beneficiaries but rather ideated in an open fashion, including all those that would improve their situation, and that of others, in the process of both designing those improvements and educating those with design skills to apply them toward collective ends. This transformational learning for designers is achievable through participation in, and experience of, what Paulo Freire (2017) called 'problem-posing' education whereby 'people teach each other, mediated by the world' – 'learning together by doing together' (Thorpe et al., 2016) in an example of 'challenge driven learning' (Mulgan et al., 2016).

The challenge for design education in delivering this learning is to find clear ways to do so within the market-centric paradigm in which we find ourselves. Answering this challenge, rather than pretending there are simply 'good' and 'bad' approaches, may be the greatest social design that we can deliver.

Bibliography

Armstrong, L., Bailey, J., Julier, G. and Kimbell, L. (2014) *Social Design futures: HEI Research and the AHRC.* Brighton: University of Brighton.

Björgvinsson, E., Ehn, P. and Hillgren, P. (2012) 'Design Things and Design Thinking: Contemporary Participatory Design Challenges', *Design Issues*, 28(3), pp. 102.

Buchanan, R. (1992) 'Wicked Problems in Design Thinking', *Design Issues*, 8(2), pp. 5-21.

Chen, D.S., Cheng, L.L., Hummels, C.C.M. and Koskinen, I. (2016) 'Social Design: An introduction', *International Journal of Design*, 10(1), pp. 1-5.

Dawood, S. (2018) 'Design most popular university choice – but graduates aren't ending up as designers', *Design Week*, 15 February. Available at: *https://www.designweek.co.uk/issues/12-18-february-2018/design-popular-university-choice-graduates-arent-endingdesigners/?cmpid=dwweekly_4767717&utm_medium=email&utm_source=newsletter&utm_campaign=dw_weekly&adg=C162374B-931B-4322-BA2F-0BB9FEEEEA11* [Accessed: 15 February 2018].

Freire, P. (1968) *Pedagogy of the Oppressed.* (First published in English by The Continuum Publishing Company 1970 and republished by .London: Penguin Classics

Gamman, L. and Thorpe, A. (2006) 'Design Against Crime As Socially Responsive Theory and Practice', Dubrovnik, Croatia: DESIGN 2006 the 9th International Design Conference.

Gamman, L. and Thorpe, A. (2011) 'Design with society: Why socially responsive design is good enough', *CoDesign* (7) pp. 217-230.

Juul-Sørensen, N. (2014) 'Designers design for the 1% – it's time to start designing for the 99%', *The Guardian*, 9 May. Available at: *https://www.theguardian.com/sustainable-business/designers-design-one-percent-sustainable-future* [Accessed: 25 January 2018].

Julier, G. (2017) *Economies of Design.* London: Sage.

Julier, G. (2013) 'From Design Culture to Design Activism', *Design and Culture*, 5(2), pp. 215-236.

Manzini, E. (2009) 'New Design Knowledge', *Design Studies*, 30 (91), pp. 4-12.

Manzini, E. (2015) *Design When Everyone Designs: An introduction to Design for Social Innovation.* Cambridge, MA: MIT Press.

Markussen, T. (2017) 'Disentangling 'the social' in social design's engagement with the public realm', *CoDesign*, 13(3) pp.160-174.

Mulgan, G. (2014) *Design in public and social innovation – what works, and what could work better*, NESTA paper. Available at: *https://www.nesta.org.uk/sites/default/files/design_in_public_and_social_innovation.pdf*

Mulgan, G., Townsley, O. and Price, A. (2016) *The challenge-driven university: how real-life problems can fuel learning*, NESTA paper. Available at: *https://www.nesta.org.uk/sites/default/files/the_challenge-driven_university.pdf*

Papanek, V. (1971) *Design for the Real World.* New York: Pantheon Books.

Rittel, H. W. J. and Webber, M. M. (1972) 'Dilemmas in a General Theory of Planning', working paper no 194, *Institute of Urban and Regional Development.* Berkeley, CA: University of California.

Thackara, J. (2006) *In the Bubble: designing in a complex world.* Cambridge, Mass: MIT.

Thorpe, A., Prendiville, A. and Oliver, K. (2016) 'Learning Together by Doing Together – Building Local Government Design Capacity Through Collaboration with Design Education' Service Design Geographies. Proceedings of the ServDes.2016 Conference, Fifth Service Design and Innovation conference.

Raising the Bar

Dr Nick de Leon
Awards Committee

In just over a century our economy has transformed from an industrial to a knowledge-based, digitally-enabled, services economy.

This transformation has affected not only the private sector but also the nature and models of provision of public services. In the UK for instance, around four fifths of industry and employment is in the service sector (ONS 2016), while industrial production represents today only 11% of GDP. Since 1900 public sector expenditure has grown from 14.4% of GDP (IFS 2015) to around 41% (ONS, 2016) with the public sector becoming the largest single provider of services and embracing a design-led approach to not only public services but to the design of policy too. The products of industrial production are increasingly product service systems and are delivered as services. Instead of selling jet engines, Rolls-Royce is selling thrust or power by the hour; IBM and Microsoft are not delivering computers but provide computing in the form of cloud services or software-as-a-service; and, with the advent of driverless cars as well as future consumer attitudes to car ownership, we see the emergence of mobility-as-a-service being embraced by every major automotive manufacturer. The economic model defined by the production and consumption of physical goods has evolved to one dominated by services which Vargo and Lush (2004) would describe as Service Dominant Logic. This is the premise that a service is the fundamental basis for all economic exchanges, and physical goods are simply a distribution mechanism for service provision. This revolution is further reinforced by digital technologies which are entirely transforming the dominant service sector and establishing new benchmarks in the business value and criticality of design, as well as applying design to innovation in business models.

In 2010 Tom Goodwin, Senior VP at Havas wrote:

> "Uber, the world's largest taxi company, owns no vehicles. Facebook, the world's most popular media owner, creates no content. Alibaba, the most valuable retailer, has no inventory. And Airbnb, the world's largest accommodation provider, owns no real estate. Something interesting is happening."

These companies are collectively worth almost a trillion dollars and it was not their technological innovation that set them on the way to becoming the dominant platform in their industry. None of them were the first in their respective markets. It was the quality of the end-to-end customer experience conceived by designers that differentiated them from their competitors. It enabled them to subsequently invest in their platform and innovate in both technology and enhancing that service experience to become so dominant. They rely on designers, just as industrial companies in the past have. However, their innovations and use of design is different. It is systemic, disruptive and interdisciplinary and that is resulting in a new set of demands and capabilities required by designers to engage in systems design, experience design, and business model innovation.

The design challenges of the 21st Century

Since the inception of the Misha Black awards, designers have raised their ambition in terms of the challenges they are seeking to engage with, from social innovation to sustainability, tackling some of the world's seemingly most intractable problems. Raising ambition means raising their capacity to dissect and diagnose complex systemic problems and in turn, understand the systemic implications of the design choices they make, and the solutions they envision.

This was evidenced at the inaugural London Design Biennale in 2016, when 27 nations came together under the bold title of "the world re-imagines the world". The national installations sought to "explore the big questions and ideas about sustainability, migration, pollution, energy, cities, and social equality." For many designers and especially those joining the profession now, their personal goals and ambitions are very much aligned with those "big questions" which reflect the UN's Sustainable Development Goals, 2030. 170 countries signed up to the 17 goals and they can only be achieved if the SDGs also become the strategic business goals of industry, not just of politicians. This will demand interdisciplinary innovation as well as political will, but it will take design, not only political rhetoric, hope and prayers to achieve them.

Transforming the public sector

Similarly, governments are facing a growing demand for public services at a time of shrinking resources, combined with increasing expectations from citizens, driven by both the complexity of their needs and rising expectations, in part fuelled by the transformation in the quality of our experience of consumer services, especially digital services. Evidence of the role of design as a means of innovating policy and public services is seen through the growth in government-sponsored innovation laboratories that use design thinking. These include Policy Lab, which is part of the UK Cabinet Office, MindLab in Denmark, GobLab (Laborotorio Gobierno) in Chile and others at both city and region level (NESTA, 2012).

The emergence of these centres is recognition that a different approach is needed to tackle this "innovation imperative" (NESTA, 2012) both for policy and services. It also follows on to the lead by the private sector in using design thinking as a tool for business strategy development (R Martin, 2009) and for product and service innovation (Spohrer and Maglio, 2008) and organisational and management innovation (Gruber and de Leon, 2015); (Boland and Collopy, 2004). Recent literature argues that linear models of policy making, public administration and service delivery cannot cope either with the 'wicked problems' of a complex world nor with the increasing demand and expectations of citizens (Colander & Kupers, 2014; Muir & Parker, 2014), so this alternative approach has to come from 'beyond policy', opening the boundaries of traditional epistemologies for public policy making and public service delivery.

Innovating design education

Designers, engineers and future leaders need to be able to not only converse but have a much deeper appreciation and understanding of each other's disciplines if they are to make a meaningful contribution to innovation for our transformed economy. Some have argued that designers need to be 'T' shaped, combining depth of expertise in the design discipline with sufficient knowledge to be able to engage with other disciplines, business, management and technology in order to advance interdisciplinary innovation.

I would argue that a shallow knowledge and capacity to converse is insufficient. It needs a real depth of understanding not only of those disciplines and the most current thinking in those fields, but also an appreciation of their epistemologies, how they go about defining problems, examining them and resolving them. The opportunities and challenges represented by new digital technologies such as AI, data science, block chain and robotics as well as the emergence of service science, smart materials, and synthetic biology need to be as familiar to designers as woods, metals and plastics were for their predecessors sixty years earlier. The design department that Sir Misha Black inherited when he joined the RCA in 1959 was entitled Woods, Metals and Plastics. In service innovation, the "product" is not the output of machine tools and factories but of organisations, and of people, so the service designer needs to understand the fields of organisational behaviour, strategy and change management as well as business model innovation.

Science, medical, engineering and business schools are transforming their academic programmes to incorporate an interdisciplinary innovation approach putting design thinking at the core of their programmes, and design schools are bringing increasing rigour to their approach to design teaching, as well as reaching into the social sciences, engineering, management and business disciplines. Design thinking courses have also become de rigueur in executive education programmes for senior managers in industry as well as government ministers and senior civil servants. As just one example, the RCA ran a full day workshop for the UK Cabinet Office sponsored by the Cabinet Office Minister Francis Maude and Sir Jeremy Heywood, Head of the Civil Service, in 2012. Over 40 ministers and senior civil servants participated.

Meanwhile the people entering design schools and the profession is changing too. Courses like IDE, GID and Service Design at the RCA are attracting experienced practitioners not just from engineering, but political scientists, anthropologists, clinicians, economists, behavioural psychologists, lawyers, finance and accounting specialists, and architects. Students from these disciplines bring new ways of thinking, new ways of learning, and a fresh and invigorating perspective to both framing problems as well as devising new solutions. The ones who are applying are also more likely to have a first class honours degree, and bring both the intellectual capability and curiosity needed for design to raise its game. Similarly schools combining engineering and design, such as the Dyson School of Design Engineering at Imperial College London are attracting highly talented undergraduates combining science and technology with creativity and design talent.

This also has important pedagogical implications for design educators as they engage with students whose education in science and technology or humanities and social science and whose approach to learning, is very different from those graduating from colleges of art and design previously. Not only are we seeing a new generation of designers who draw upon other disciplines, but we need a new generation of educators whose pedagogical approach is adaptive and agile to their needs, and is drawn from other specialisations.

Conclusion

The nature of the problems designers are tackling has changed, as has their ambition to engage in bigger issues than making products look good or reducing the costs of products through design. We have seen the decline in industrial production and consumption and the corresponding growth in private as well as public sector service provision and consumption, and this is compounded by greater empowerment and expectations of the overall service experience by customers and citizens. The primacy in design of customer experience and an understanding of not just technical systems but complex social, economic, political and cultural systems has become crucial for designers. This is resulting in designers requiring distinctly different skills and backgrounds.

If design is to fulfil its ambition to tackle the bigger issues, it has to change and that starts with the intellectual capability of those coming into the profession, the technical development of its current practitioners, and the enhancing and enriching capacity of future generations of design educators.

Bibliography

Boland, RJ. Collopy, F. 2004. *Managing as Designing.* Stanford University Press. Stanford, CA, USA

Brown, T. 2008. Design thinking. *Harvard Business Review*, 86: 84–92, 141.

Colander, D, Kupers, R. 2014. Complexity and the Art of Public Policy. *Journal of Economic Literature,* 54(2): 534-72.

Gruber, M; de Leon, N. 2015. Managing by Design. *Academy of Management Journal* 2015, Vol. 58, No. 1, 1–7.

Institute of Fiscal Studies. 2015. Public Expenditure Growth. *https://www.ifs.org.uk/tools_and_resources/fiscal_facts/public_spending_survey/total_public_spending*

Muir, R. Parker, I. 2014. *Many to Many – How the relational state will transform public services.* Institute for Public Policy Research, February 2014.

Martin, R. 2009 *The design of business: why design thinking is the next competitive advantage,* Harvard Business Press.

NESTA. Christiansen, J. Bunt, L. 2014 *Innovation in policy:allowing for creativity, social complexity and uncertainty in public governance.* NESTA Publication. October 2012

Office of National Statistics: Employment and Labour Market *https://www.ons.gov.uk/employmentandlabourmarket/peopleinwork/employmentandemployeetypes*

Office of National Statistics, 2016: UK Perspectives, 25 March 2016 *http://webarchive.nationalarchives.gov.uk/20170726163558/http://visual.ons.gov.uk/introducing-uk-perspectives-2016/*

Spohrer J, Maglio PP. 2004. The emergence of service science: Toward systematic service innovations to accelerate co creation of value. Production and Operations Management 17 (3), 238-246.

Vargo, S.L. and Lusch, R.L. (2004) 'Evolving to a New Dominant Logic for Marketing', *Journal of Marketing 68* (1): 1–17

World Bank. 2016 *http://data.worldbank.org/indicator/NV.IND.MANF.ZS?locations=GB*

On Engineering and Design

Professor Geoffrey Kirk RDI
Medallist 2006

Engineering courses have changed and developed in response to business and society's needs and they will continue to evolve to meet future demands.

When Sir Misha Black was Professor of Industrial Design at the Royal College of Art, there were two routes for an engineering education. Universities offered courses in Applied or Engineering Science. The Colleges of Advanced Technology and Technical Colleges offered rather more focussed courses in particular branches of engineering – for example, mechanical, electrical or production. Both routes eventually led to membership of an appropriate professional institution. In most courses exposure to the design process was limited to producing a design where the requirements were known, the methods of achieving those requirements were well established and the outcome could be pre-determined – a process which required little creativity. They were exercises in analysis of existing mechanisms or systems.

Changes had to be made in response to a number of factors. There was an increasing rate of technology improvement, pressure on industry for better quality, better value, faster time to market and improved return on investment. Products and manufacturing processes were becoming increasingly complex requiring more interdisciplinary activity and team-working. This increased complexity required better communication and presentation skills. There was increasing pressure to produce environmentally sustainable products requiring designers to address the whole life cycle. There was also the desire to improve the regulation of engineers in the United Kingdom.

In 1981 the Engineering Council was established by Royal Charter to define the standards for engineering professionalism. It also published and publishes the learning outcomes, via the UK Spec, that have to be met by degree programmes for the award of Engineering Council accreditation, which largely limits membership of the professional institutions to holders of those degrees. The UK Spec has continually been revised in response to changing circumstances.

The UK Spec attaches a great importance to the design process – establishing requirements, creativity, rational decision-making, embodiment and delivery. This is because design teaching delivers many of the skills and attributes required by engineers. Foremost, it promotes both analytical and creative thinking which is at the centre of effective design. It emphasises constructive reasoning to achieve objective assessments of issues and optimum outcomes. It encourages the communication and team-working essential in modern industry. To achieve many of these outcomes it has to be multidisciplinary, for example combining mechanics with electronics and new production methods with material technology. Some students may have no intention of becoming designers but they will use the process in research, planning or managing design teams. The delivery of the curriculum in most courses is met by lectures on the design process. In each year students have Group Design, Make and Test projects and Individual Feasibility Studies, that link theory and practice. A key objective of these exercises is for the students to have the opportunity to create numerous options and to make rational choices between them. So the requirements and methods for achieving them are not predetermined, making the outcomes indeterminate. The tasks become more challenging and complex as the student progresses.

The importance placed on engineering design education by the accreditation bodies resulted in many excellent developments during the 1980s in university engineering departments. The Royal Academy of Engineering recognised the need to maintain this momentum. However it became increasingly difficult to recruit academic staff with experience of engineering design in industry, which prompted the Academy to launch the Visiting Professors in Engineering Design initiative.

The principles of design are to some extent universal but the methods and tools will change with the development of greater computational capability, and advanced manufacturing techniques. Also the role of designers is likely to change in the future. Designers have always striven to create artefacts, systems and processes with the materials and technology available at the time. In future designers will have to conceive products where the question becomes not 'what can be achieved with what is available?' but 'what technology is needed to meet the targets?' This leads to designers having a wider role in defining technology acquisition targets. These changes will undoubtedly need to be considered in future curricula.

Sir Misha Black championed increasing the engineering content in arts education, and the arts content in engineering education, and engineering education has indeed over the years embraced many of the attributes inherent in arts education – bringing the two closer together with the common aim of excellence in design.

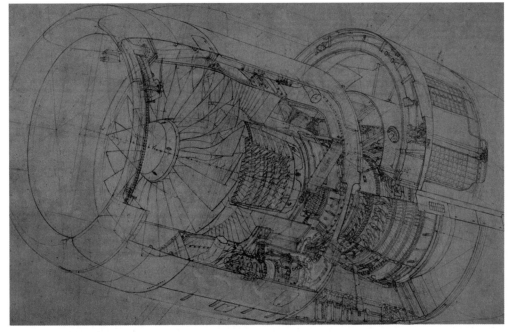

Isometric drawing for the Rolls-Royce RB211-535E4 jet engine, early 1980s.

A Larger Reality

Professor Anthony Dunne
Award 2009

"When life itself seems lunatic, who knows where madness lies? Perhaps to be too practical is madness. To surrender dreams – this may be madness. Too much sanity may be madness – and maddest of all: to see life as it is, and not as it should be!"
Miguel de Cervantes Saavedra's Don Quixote in *Man of La Mancha* by Dale Wasserman (1965).

Writing about design education at a time when in the West we are experiencing a major reconfiguring of geopolitical power relations and a shift towards inward-looking nationalism; the marketisation of seemingly every aspect of life, including education; increasing environmental instability and uncertainty; and the appearance of significant cracks in a political and economic system that, while generating vast wealth, has completely failed to ensure its fair distribution; it is hard to be optimistic. But I will try.

What if our approach to design education is wrong? What if educating designers to work with prevailing economic, social, technological and political realities – designing for how the world is now, has become a convenient conceit? What if teaching student designers to frame every issue, no matter how complex, as a problem to be solved squanders valuable creative and imaginative energy on the unachievable? What if design education's focus on 'making stuff real' perpetuates everything that is wrong with current reality, ensuring that all possible futures are merely extrapolations of a dysfunctional present?

If for a moment we were to abandon the tried and tested approaches of Western design education, approaches designed and built in the twentieth century but struggling to adapt to the realities of the twenty-first, where would the search for alternatives begin?

For me, it would have to be with the idea of reality, or more precisely, The Real, and how it is dealt with in Western design pedagogy, especially in relation to emerging technology. With few exceptions, at the heart of most current approaches to design education is a zealous focus on being realistic. By thinking within existing realities whether social, political, economic or technological, the ideas, beliefs and values that have gotten us into this very difficult situation are reproduced through design, endlessly. Yet the underlying logic driving the labelling of certain ideals, hopes and dreams as real and others as unreal is rarely challenged or even questioned, leading to the ongoing suppression of the design imagination.

As the current geopolitical situation is making very clear, just because something is impossible, does not mean it is not possible. In this light, it might be more realistic if design education prepared designers to be what writer Ursula K. Le Guin has called 'realists of a larger reality'. A reality that fully embraces the imagination and all that is yet to exist, or might never exist – what we currently think of as unreality.

Such an education would encourage designers to be constructively unrealistic. But to do this, it would be necessary to embrace new ways of thinking that break with conventional wisdom and begin to experiment with other kinds of wisdom, much of which may feel

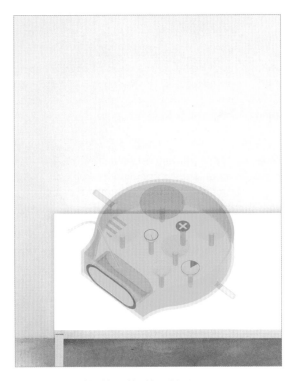

Ethiculator from *Not Here, Not Now*, 2014

The Ethiculator is a calculator for resolving everyday ethical dilemmas. It is one of six studies for fictional digital products, each accompanied only by a title that hinted at its function and purpose, commissioned for the Future Fiction exhibition at Z33 in Hasselt in 2014.

counter-intuitive or even unpalatable.

One thing design does very well is give tangible form to ideas, ideals, attitudes, and ways of seeing the world, all expressed through the stuff of everyday life. But the kinds of stories currently being projected through Western design are pretty disheartening. A narrow range of technological narratives dominates the Western design imagination. Expressed through idealised products, services and scenarios, they focus on celebrating unfettered consumption and technological progress; economic growth regardless of cost to the planet, people and other species; denial of impending environmental doom; and the facilitation of a technologically mediated form of group-think. They are so prevalent that it is becoming increasingly difficult to imagine other possibilities. But this is exactly what we need to do – to imagine radically different ways of being. Ways of being, currently deemed unrealistic.

Whole new worlds are imagined by writers, film-makers, and artists. Could this approach be integrated into design education so design schools could become a source of alternative ideas and counter narratives, materialised through design, that provoke thought and further imagining about the kind of worlds people wish to live in rather than prescribing any one particular future or communicating a vision of how things will, or should be?

A design education like this would probably no longer be organised around disciplines but instead, maybe, different ways of seeing the world. Its students and faculty would study, experiment with, and deepen understanding of the mechanics of unreality – utopias, dystopias and heterotopias; what ifs and as ifs; hypotheses, thought experiments and reductio ad absurdum; counterfactuals and uchronia, and so on. Synthesising ideas from political science, anthropology, sociology, history, economics and philosophy into new worldviews made tangible through an expanded form of design practice.

From where we stand today, this might seem unrealistic, maybe even a little escapist, so I will end by turning once again to Ursula K. Le Guin and her response to critiques of highly imaginative work as escapism: "The direction of escape is toward freedom. So what is 'escapism' an accusation of?"

Age : The Challenge for Design

Professor Roger Coleman
Award 2001

This paper was presented at the Design Renaissance Congress, Glasgow, September 1993

First World populations are living longer. The over-50s have growing economic power. Yet stereotypical views of age confuse design for an ageing population with design for disability and special needs. New product strategies are needed to produce better solutions for people of all ages.

In the 1960s we simply did not consider the possibility of being old one day. The reasons for this could lie in the fact that until as recently as 1950 the probability of our surviving to enjoy any significant period of retirement was low. Consequently there was no advantage in anticipating a lengthy 'old age'. After 1950, however, things began to change and now four out of every ten adults is over 50. 'My generation' and those who follow now have to confront longevity. Time has caught up with us.

My earlier understanding of age reflected my parents' idea that it was a relatively short period of slippers-by-the-fire, of the bent back and walking stick of the road sign used by *The Oldie* magazine in its logo. (Incidentally the road sign is a designer's view of age, not an old person's.) Age was something akin to a rainy day that one saved up against, and the dominant view of age is still framed in such pre-war terms. That is why, when most designers talk about design and older people, they assume that means designing for people with disabilities or special needs. That is why, when the caring professions talk about 'the elderly', they can do so in ways that suggest all old people are dependent and living in institutions when more that 95 per cent of over-50s live at home; and when gerontologists talk about old people, their professional or academic objectivity can reinforce a them-and-us view which makes it difficult to acknowledge that old people are simply ourselves in the future.

Too many people carry that road sign around in their heads. It is what they think of when they think 'old', and it brings with it a patronising and complacent mythology which is utterly inappropriate to a world in which the old are rapidly outnumbering the young. What we need instead are new models of age; models of independent, active life (physical, mental and economic); models that acknowledge the diversity and talents of our ageing population; models that liberate rather than restrict. Above all, we need models that recognise our adult potential as active and contributing to society for a period extending across 60 or more years.

This is a great challenge to us all, and design has a vital role to play here as enabler, shaping a world that is user-friendly, flexible and accommodating, that adjusts to our changing capabilities as we age, and offers us a chance to adapt by remaining active and fit for as long as possible. This challenge was taken up by the Royal College of Art when, with the support of the Helen Hamlyn Foundation and Safeway plc, it launched an action-research programme exploring the implications for design and communication of the ageing of populations across the First World. I am privileged to lead the Design Age programme at the RCA: age is perhaps the design challenge of the future.

Design which reinforces stereotypes

As a judge of the New Design for Old section of the RSA Student Design Awards in Britain, I see a high proportion of entries each year falling into the gadget category – gadgets for opening doors, gadgets for opening jars, add-ons and adaptations. These aids, often ingenious, address the fact that many everyday objects make life difficult for anyone who is less than able-bodied. But they still inevitably stigmatise the user and they reinforce the 'old equals infirm' stereotype. What I don't see enough of are things I can't wait to own, and what I am all too aware of is that so many things need redesigning and rethinking if they are to work well for people of all ages.

It is my belief that if we design with the needs of older people, of ourselves in the future, in mind at every step of the process then we will arrive at products which work better for everybody, regardless of age or ability. And it is important to remember that when it comes to infrastructure – buildings, roads, stations, rolling stock and so on – we are talking about things which may last as long as we do: if we design these things for ourselves at age 30 we may find that they do not work for us at 70. This is an important point, because older people are not a different species; they are quite simply ourselves in the future.

But what point is there in thinking in this way if we can only see the negative side of age, if we can only see it as something to be avoided and postponed? My answer is that this view of age is so dominant because, like the road sign, it was framed in the past. Today's reality is very different. At the end of the nineteenth century the majority of the UK population was aged under 30, and the proportion surviving to 70 tiny. Then it would have been unreasonable to anticipate anything other than a short retirement: a period of rest after a lifetime of work. One hundred years later, things are very different. Life expectation has increased by 50 per cent during this century. Four out of ten British voters are already over 50, and by 2021 the over 50s are likely to hold a majority.

The process we are involved in constitutes a radical and probably irreversible shift away from youth-dominated societies. Understanding it will involve a complete rethink of what age means, and as we undertake that, we will be forced to draw a new map of life in which the 30 or more years we can look forward to after the age of 50 will be as important to us as the 30 years before.

In many senses 50 can now be regarded as the centre of gravity of our adult lives. If we are to enjoy the new lease of life that implies, we will need to see enormous changes in the design of everyday objects and environments. That in itself is a considerable challenge to design, but I believe the bigger and really exciting challenge is to begin to conceive of a world that is radically different and infinitely more user-friendly than the world we inhabit at the moment. New technology offers us the ability to make big changes, but the uses we make of it will be shaped by how we see ourselves in the future.

Drive of the marketplace

Of course, it would be naive to suggest that the sort of changes I have suggested will come about without the commercial drive of the marketplace. According to Danielle Barr, director of Third Age Marketing, people over 50 have more disposable income than any other population group. The economic power of this group is quite formidable: they account for 30 per cent of all consumer expenditure – over £30 billion – and account for 60 per cent of all savings. Yet there is very little evidence of this economic power in the marketplace because this group are ignored by marketing.

Consequently, says Barr, they are becoming angry and frustrated by the irony that even though they have the time and the money to spend, there are not many things that appeal to them. Many more products and designs actually irritate them because they are so poorly designed ergonomically. Danielle Barr suggests a reason for the slowness to change: marketing departments, advertising agencies and design consultancies are, on the whole, staffed by young people. The average age of a brand manager is 29. Agency creative teams are often even younger.

Shifting from margin to mainstream

Nine months in 1988 saw the confirmation of the ozone hole, the publication of the *Green Consumer Guide*, Mrs Thatcher's pro-environment speech, and an intensive media campaign orchestrated by a relatively small group of committed individuals and organisations. By the end of that year, environmentalism was here to stay and most major companies now regard environment as a competitive factor. That dramatic shift from margin to mainstream took the design community, and in particular design education, by surprise. So, as age moves onto the mainstream agenda, I think it is vitally important that we in the design community are prepared and up to speed.

The first step is to recognise that this is a new and uncharted area. Just as older people lack positive role models, we are also lacking in examples of age-friendly design – although pioneers like Maria Benkzton of Egonomi Design Gruppen in Sweden have worked for 20 years on user-friendly design for disability which provides solutions that work better for people of all ages.

Developing an understanding of older users, in the sense of well-researched ergonomics, is clearly one key to a user-friendly future. Another is understanding the needs and aspirations of older people, and one way of doing this is to try and see the world 'through other eyes'. Age Concern England is now running courses in which participants can begin to find out what it feels like to be older. The programme originated in Canada and has proved very successful in helping decision-makers appreciate how they can improve the provision they make for older customers.

Innovation most often comes about when we change our viewpoint and look at things anew. The changing age-profile of First World nations allows us a unique opportunity to question the way we have designed in the past, and to approach the future from a different perspective. In doing this we are all treading new ground and so are unlikely to get everything right, but it is very important that we explore the widest range of options in the most imaginative way. If we don't, then we can all look forward to an extended and very dull old age.

Deeper and Wider

Professor Rachel Cooper OBE
Award 2015

In order to think about the future of design education, it is worth putting it into the context of the past. When I began my undergraduate degree in multidisciplinary design in 1973 at North Staffordshire Polytechnic, this course was seen as rather a radical approach compared to conventional design education based in discipline silos such as graphic design, industrial design, fashion and interiors etc. In most universities design research did not exist, other than as the historical and theory aspects of design education. Misha Black, Bruce Archer and John Christopher Jones had of course been pioneering design methods and design research in the sixties. But to young aspiring designers in the 1970s we were still eager to train in design practice and get a job.

In the following 40 years, design education has changed considerably, first driven by forces in the education system such as the move to university status for many polytechnics (where art and design tended to reside), the research assessment exercise, resulting in an increasing focus on research and on higher degrees (PhDs). This meant that more funding was available for design research in what is known as a dual support system, whereby universities are funded based on the excellence of their research and where the UK research councils offer competitive research opportunities to all disciplines including design.

The second driving force was the changing nature of design, both within universities and outside them. Design Management as a discipline led by Michael Farr and Peter Gorb in the 1970s widened the opportunity base for research and practice both in education and industry, followed by the application of design to services (1990s), and more recently towards policy (2000s). At the same time, global challenges around sustainability, climate change, and health and wellbeing have meant that design has partnered with scientists and social scientists to research and deliver potential solutions and interventions.

We now have a well-established design research community, especially in the UK. We have highly ranked journals in design and a significant publishing record. However, there has always been a tension in education between a concern to develop the discipline – to build its research credibility against the other sciences – whilst retaining the pragmatic and practical education environment that prepares design students for practice in industry. In effect, this is tension between practice and wider intellectual enquiry. Indeed in a recent research study[1] there was a difference between what academics and practitioners valued in design education: for instance academics, whilst still valuing design skills, saw a transformation of design sustained by the idea of design being less a making and styling discipline and more a thinking and research discipline. Practitioners on the other hand placed more stress on aesthetic sensibility and expertise, understanding the design process, functionalism, consumerism and client-designer relationships. In general terms, companies are adopting the understanding and

---

[1] The Value of Design in Innovation: results from a survey within the UK Industry, Hernandez, R. J., Cooper, R., Tether, B. & Murphy, E. L. 6/09/2017 In : The Design Journal. 20 , Suppl. 1, p. S691-S704 14 p.

applications of design commonly found in research, but at a less accelerated rate than in academic environments.

Design education has always been a source of innovation – many graduates go on to careers driving the development of new products and services across all sectors of industry – and it must continue to challenge the 'skills need' demand over innovation in education and research. Today the horizon for design education has widened. Design education is now built not only on the innovation needs of industry, but on the insights arising from research that has been undertaken in large multidisciplinary groups, addressing for instance, design for health and wellbeing, or design against crime, or design for future mobilities.

" New materials and new technologies mean that the future of design education is vast. Design education must be deeper and wider."

Now the rapid changes in society that are being driven by trends in technology, especially in new materials and new digital technologies such as Artificial Intelligence, Augmented and Virtual Reality enhanced by data science, means that the future of design education is vast. Design education must be deeper and wider; there will be designers whose titles bear no resemblance to the old categories of graphics, product, fashion etc. The choice of design education will be greater. There will be more graduate level design apprenticeships, enabling industry-based responsive education; there will be more joint programmes around materials, computer sciences and design, as well as health and behavioural sciences, all based on excellence in research. It is clear that we will continue to need the visualisation, making, imaginative, complex and holistic thinking skills that good design education provides, so that the next generation of designers can be leaders in addressing the challenges facing society and indeed the world, in the next forty years and beyond.

College of Medallists 1978–2018

1978
Sir William Coldstream CBE
1908–1987

Born in Northumberland, William Coldstream grew up in London and studied at the Slade School of Art, University College London. In 1937 he co-founded the Euston Road School with Graham Bell and others, and with the outbreak of the Second World War was enlisted in the Royal Artillery, but was later appointed War Artist, painting in Egypt and Italy.

Coldstream's reputation as an influential art and design educator was crystallised in 1958 when he became Chairman of the National Advisory Council on Art Education, a position he held until 1971. Under his chairmanship, British art (and design) education were radically restructured. Having worked alongside John Grierson of the GPO Film Unit in the 1930s, Coldstream became Chairman of the British Film Institute (BFI) from 1964 to 1971. Coldstream was made CBE in 1952, and was knighted in 1956.

1980
Serge Ivan Chermayeff Hon RDI
1900–1986

Serge Ivan Chermayeff was born in Grozny, Azerbaijan, and moved to England at an early age. In 1931 Chermayeff formed his own architectural firm where, in 1933, he was joined by German architect Erich Mendelsohn. As Members of the Modern Architectural Research Group (MARS), together they created some of the most important works in the British Modern Movement, notably the De La Warr Pavilion, Bexhill on Sea (1935) and Cohen House, London (1936).

In 1940, Chermayeff emigrated to the United States where he began to teach at the California School of Fine Arts. After moving to New York City, Chermayeff became Professor of Art at Brooklyn College and in 1946 Director of the Institute of Design in Chicago. He continued to teach at several universities including Massachusetts Institute of Technology (MIT), Harvard and Yale. Chermayeff was awarded honorary degrees from numerous colleges and universities.

1982
Max Bill
1908–1994

Max Bill was born in Winterthur, Switzerland. In 1927, Bill took up studies at the Bauhaus in Dessau. After moving to Zurich in 1952, Bill, Inge Aicher-Scholl and Otl Aicher founded the Ulm School of Design, with Bill as principal and Head of the Department for Architecture and Product Form. While teaching at Ulm, Bill was also having a decisive influence on graphic design through his theoretical writings and progressive work. His work was characterised by its clarity of design and precise proportions, such as his design 'Ulmer Hocker' – a stool that can also be used as a shelf element or a side table. Bill was a member of the Swiss National Council, he became an associate member of the Royal Flemish Academy of Science, Literature and Fine Art in Brussels and a member of the Berlin Academy of Arts.

1985
Ashoke Chatterjee

Ashoke Chatterjee was executive director of National Institute of Design (NID) from 1975-85, and thanks to his input, the NID in Ahmedabad became internationally recognised as India's foremost institution in the field of design education, research and training. Chatterjee later became Senior Faculty Advisor for Design Management and Communication from 1985 to 1995, and a Distinguished Fellow at NID from 1995 until his retirement in 2001. For many years, he served as honorary president of the Crafts Council of India, and worked as a consultant in India and internationally, particularly on projects concerned with water management and environmental issues. After more than ten years as international advisor, in 2000 Chatterjee joined the board of directors of Aid to Artisans, a US based non-profit organisation offering practical assistance to artisans worldwide.

1986
Frank Height
1921–2013

Frank Height was Professor Emeritus of Industrial Design, and successor to Sir Misha Black at the Royal College of Art. He was a Fellow of the Royal Academy of Engineering, the Institution of Mechanical Engineers, the Chartered Society of Designers and the Royal Society of Arts. He was recipient of many awards including three Design Council awards; the Silver Medal XII Triennale, Milan; international design awards in Paris, Hanover and New York; and the Institute of Packaging Award. Professor Height's professional work included the design of furniture, plastics, domestic products, medical equipment, office equipment and business machines, and interiors and exhibitions.

1988
Peter Reyner Banham
1922–1988

Peter Reyner Banham studied at the Courtauld Institute of Art, London. Banham had connections with the gathering of intellectuals and artists known as the Independent Group (IG), which staged the pioneering 1956 art exhibition *This Is Tomorrow*, considered by many to be the birth of Pop Art. From the mid 1970s, primarily living in the United States, Banham went on to become a prolific architecture critic and writer. Banham is best known for his 1960 theoretical treatise *Theory and Design in the First Machine Age*. His other great work is *Los Angeles: The Architecture of Four Ecologies*. Banham predicted a "second age" of the machine and mass consumption building on Giedion's *Mechanization Takes Command* (1948). As a professor, Banham taught at the University of London, the State University of New York, Buffalo, and through the 1980s at the University of California, Santa Cruz. He was appointed the Sheldon H. Solow Professor of the History of Architecture at the Institute of Fine Arts, New York University shortly before his death.

1991
David Pye

David William Pye studied at the Architectural Association in London. His main career was in teaching and he spent 26 years at the Royal College of Art, London (1948-1974), for the last decade of which he was Professor of Furniture Design. Pye was an acclaimed writer on craft and design – his *The Nature and Aesthetics of Design* (1964) was followed by *The Nature and Art of Workmanship* (1968), which introduced the concept of "the workmanship of risk" and had a profound influence on craft-practice. Throughout his career, Pye designed furniture for industrial production, and also crafted turned wooden bowls and boxes. He exhibited and sold his work continuously from 1949 to the early 1980s and in 1984–5 the Crafts Council arranged a touring retrospective exhibition of his work. In 1985 he was awarded an OBE.

1993
Dr Marianne Straub RDI
1909–1992

Born in the village of Amriswil, Switzerland, Marianne Straub attended art school in Zürich where she studied weaving under Bauhaus-trained Heinz Otto Hurlimann. She moved to England to study at Bradford Technical College where she was the third female student ever to have been enrolled. She became one of the leading commercial designers of textiles in Britain throughout the 1940s, 50s and 60s.

In the 1950s, Straub was closely associated with the north Essex village of Great Bardfield, which became famous for its small community of talented artists through "open house" exhibitions of the Great Bardfield Artists, which attracted national press attention and thousands of visitors. As well as her design work, Straub was an important teacher of textile design, having begun teaching at the Central School of Art, London in 1956. She later taught at Hornsey College of Art before moving on to the Royal College of Art, where she worked for many years. She provided a living link between Bauhaus textiles and modern production techniques.

1993
Arthur Pulos
1917–1997

Born in North Vandergrift, Arthur Pulos was an industrial designer, scholar, author and founder of Pulos Design Associates. From 1946 to 1955 he was Associate Professor of Design at the University of Illinois and continued his academic career with a move to Syracuse University, where he was appointed chairman of the Department of Design. Pulos wrote *Opportunities in Industrial Design* and then his two-part masterpiece *American Design Ethic* (1983) and *American Design Adventure* (1988). In addition, Pulos was a practising industrial designer, and was a founding member and the last president of Industrial Designers Education Association (IDEA), and was a former President of the International Council of Societies of Industrial Design (ICSID).

1995
Kenji Ekuan
1929–2015

Born in Tokyo in 1929, Kenji Ekuan was a prominent Japanese designer and founder of the core group that became GK Design. Towards the end of World War II he moved to Hiroshima where he witnessed the atomic bombing of the city, which motivated him to become a 'creator of things'. As well as his inspirational design practice, in 1970 Ekuan became president of the Japan Industrial Designers' Association and five years later he was elected as president of the International Council of Societies of Industrial Design. He served as Chair of the Japan Institute of Design, was Dean of Shizuoka University of Art and Culture and a trustee of the Art Center College of Design.

Ekuan understood design as a source for improving the quality of life and emphasised that objects always need to have a certain spirit alongside functionality in order to be used with pleasure and not just as mere "tools".

1997
Dr Alexander Moulton RDI
1920–2012

Dr Alexander Moulton was the innovative engineering designer and inventor who developed a rubber suspension system for vehicles – notably BMC's Mini and British Leyland cars – which were to have a profound impact on transport design. He went on to design his classic Moulton bicycle – combining small wheels, rubber suspension and sturdy engineering – which revolutionised cycling at a time when it was becoming increasingly popular (because environmentally friendly). Some fifty years after the introduction of the first commercial model, his design has continued to maintain its influence and success. Alexander Moulton became an RDI in 1968.

1998
William H. Walsh
1915–1999

In 1963 an initiative took place which was to change how the Irish – government, industry, education and training – related to design. It was led by William H Walsh, then head of the Irish Export Board. The purpose was to inspire Irish industry (up to then tariff protected and inward looking) to improve their products through appropriate and good deign and make goods which were desirable in international markets, create jobs at home, revive skills and by example and input create a climate in which educational establishments would raise their standards so that young Irish people might be trained as designers. His vision and the achievements of the Kilkenny Design Workshops underpinned the successful design profession and a new visual awareness in Ireland, both so evident today.

1999
Ettore Sottsass Hon RDI
1917–2007

Born in Innsbruck, Austria, but growing up in Milan, Sottsass graduated from Politecnico di Torino in Turin with a degree in architecture. Sottsass designed iconic products for Olivetti, which included ELEA 9003, the first Italian mainframe computer which won him Italy's highest design award in 1959, as well as the bright red Pop Art inspired Olivetti Valentine typewriter he designed with Perry King in 1969. He is best known as the founder of the early 1980s Memphis collective, a group of international architects hailed as one of the most characteristic examples of Post-modernism in design and the arts. As an industrial designer, Sottsass's clients included Fiorucci, Esprit, the Italian furniture company Poltronova, Knoll International, and Alessi. As an architect, he designed the Mayer-Schwarz Gallery on Rodeo Drive in Beverly Hills, California, with its dramatic doorway made of irregular folds and jagged angles..

2000
Professor Richard Guyatt CBE
1914–2007

A British graphic designer and academic, Richard Guyatt has been described as 'one of the 20th century's most seminal figures in the world of graphic design'. Richard Guyatt was the youngest-ever professor at the Royal College of Art, where he helped to re-launch the institution after the second world war as a place that prepared students for lives in the specialised design professions – through teaching by active design – rather than as career academics. He also popularised the term "graphic design" and expanded the curriculum to include graphics, typography, illustration, printmaking, photography, film and television design. His own graphics spanned posters, packaging and advertising. In 1969, Guyatt was made a Commander of the British Empire (CBE).

2000
Robert Goodden RDI

Robert Goodden trained as an architect at the Architectural Association and was a key figure in the resurgence of British design in the period after the Second World War. In 1946 Goodden was at work on *Britain Can Make It*, the first large-scale peacetime design exhibition, held at the V&A. His role was even more significant at the 1951 Festival of Britain, where alongside Richard Guyatt and Dick Russell, he designed the Lion & Unicorn Pavilion. At the forefront of the post-war "homes for the people" movement, Goodden was a member of the Utility Furniture Committee, chaired by Gordon Russell, and then joined Gordon's brother RD Russell in architectural partnership in London. As professor of silversmithing and jewellery at the Royal College of Art from 1948 to 1974, Goodden nurtured several generations of metalwork designers and craftspeople.

2001
Yuri Soloviev
1920–2013

Yuri Soloviev studied design in Moscow in 1938, before going on to work as a designer in a number of state-funded enterprises. Charged with expanding design activity in the USSR, Soloviev was appointed Director of the government-sponsored Research Institute of Industrial Design VNIITE (1962-87). VNIITE grew in size and significance with branch offices across Russia establishing international relationships through the organisation of exhibitions and seminars. One of the leading figures in design in the USSR in the second half of the 20th century, Soloviev worked in many fields including furniture, interior, industrial, and transport design. In addition, Soloviev disseminated his ideas widely through his editorship from 1964 onwards of the Tekniecheskaya Estetika (Technical Aesthetic) VNIITE design journal, and through his many publications. His importance was recognised by many design awards including the fourth Osaka International Design Award, the International World Design Prize, and the Japan Design Foundation's International Design Award.

2002
Dr Santiago Calatrava

Born in Benimàmet, Spain, Calatrava graduated in Architecture at the Polytechnic University of Valencia and remained at the university to take a postgraduate course in Urbanism. Many view Calatrava's design work as situated at the junction between art, architecture and engineering, changing the shape of architectural design and acting as an inspiration for future generations of students. His best-known work, in the form of bridges and towers, is closely related to his own drawings of the human body and to his sculptures of geometric forms, inspired by the dynamics of movement and tension. His most famous projects including the urban regeneration of Stadelhofen Station in Zurich (1983-90), the birdlike forms of the TGV Station and Airport at Lyons-Satolas (1989-94), Trinity Bridge, Salford (1992-95), the Oriente Station, Lisbon (1993-98) and the City of Science, Valencia (1991-2001).

2003
Professor Sir Christopher Frayling

Sir Christopher Frayling read history at Churchill College, Cambridge where he later gained a PhD in the study of Jean-Jacques Rousseau's ideas on art education. Joining London's Royal College of Art in 1973, at first part-time, Frayling founded the Department of Cultural History, and from 1996 to 2009 was Rector and Vice-Provost of the college. As Professor of Cultural History, he instituted pioneering new courses on the History of Design, the Conservation of artefacts and Curating Contemporary Art. Frayling's achievements and honours are numerous. He has been awarded honorary doctorates by nine universities in the UK and in 2001, was granted a knighthood for "Services to Art and Design Education". Other prominent roles have included Chairman of the Design Council, Chairman of the Royal Mint Advisory Committee, Trustee of the Victoria & Albert Museum, Patron of the Robin and Lucienne Day Foundation, and between 2004 and 2007 Chairman of the Arts Council England. Outside design circles, Christopher Frayling is known for his wide output as a writer, broadcaster and critic, especially on film, popular culture and design.

2004
Professor David Hamilton (Honorary)

David Hamilton was awarded the Medal for his services to the Sir Misha Black Awards Committee. He was born and educated in Yorkshire. He attended the Regional College of Art in Bradford where he studied Painting & Pottery for the National Diploma in Design. In 1974 Hamilton was appointed Head of Ceramics at the Royal College of Art in the School of Ceramics & Glass led by Professor David Lord Queensberry. He became Professor of Ceramics & Glass RCA in 1984, and under his guidance the department stressed both design for industry and artist-craftmanship. In the 1980s he undertook several public art commissions notably Parsons Polygon in Newcastle upon Tyne and Station Identity schemes at Paddington and Euston Northern Line underground stations for London Underground. He has written widely on the art, craft, design and technology of ceramics for international journals and magazines.

2004
Elaine Ostroff

Elaine Ostroff started her career in design education in 1961, founding the *Looking Glass Theatre* in Providence, Rhode Island. Her work with children at the theatre encouraged the transformation of institutional educational environments in the USA. Later in the decade, Ostroff played a key role in establishing a multi-disciplinary graduate programme at the Massachusetts College of Art that emphasised the role of designers and artists in creating community-based projects for disabled people. Ostroff continued her pioneering work in 1978 when she co-founded the Adaptive Environments Centre in Boston Massachusetts. In 1992, Ostroff set up the Universal Design Education Project, working with faculty from 25 colleges and universities across the United States. Other major projects include founding the Global Universal Design Educators Network, as well as co-editing the Universal Design Handbook, which was published by McGraw-Hill in 2001.

2005
Professor David Kelley

Born in Barberton, Ohio, United States, David Kelley trained in electrical engineering at Carnegie Mellon University. Frustrated by the many barriers to innovation in the field of engineering, Kelley applied to Stanford University to study product design. David Kelley became a professor at Stanford University in 1991, and was later named Donald W. Whittier Professor of Mechanical Engineering. One of America's leading advocates of human-centered design, through his teaching at Stanford, as well as his continuing role as Chairman of IDEO, he has been greatly influential in moving the disciplines of engineering and design much closer together. Building on this legacy, in 2004 Kelley founded the Hasso Plattner Institute of Design at Stanford. One of the world's most innovative design teachers, Professor David Kelley has received numerous awards including the Chrysler Design Award, the Smithsonian's National Design Award in Product Design, and the Edison Achievement Award by the Thomas Edison Papers at Rutgers University.

2006
Professor Geoffrey Kirk RDI

Geoffrey Kirk joined Rolls-Royce at their Derby branch in 1968. He was for 30 years Rolls-Royce's Chief Design Engineer for Civil Aerospace. During Kirk's long career at Rolls-Royce, major achievements included his conceptual design for the Trent 500, the sole power plant used in the Airbus A340-500/600 aircraft, and the Trent 900 for the Airbus A380, as well as leading the team responsible for designing the original version of the Trent 1000. Having left Rolls-Royce, Kirk embarked on a career in design education in which he assisted UK educational institutions in fostering that same excellence of advanced engineering design and skills he had previously pioneered. He is a Visiting Professor at Queen Mary, University of London and the University of Nottingham and a member of the Design Council. Kirks list of honours includes the Prince Philip Designers Prize, Fellow of the Royal Academy of Engineering (FREng), and Royal Designer for Industry (RDI).

2007
Alison Chitty OBE RDI

Alison Chitty began her career after graduating from St Martins School of Art in London in the early 1970s. From 1979 she began working on productions for the Hampstead Theatre, Riverside Studios, the Royal Shakespeare Company and in the West End, later becoming resident designer at the Royal National Theatre. Her design work came to be highly regarded within the worlds of stage and screen. She worked on the production design for Award-winning films, including *Secrets and Lies*. Chitty won an Olivier award for Best Costume Designer for *Remembrance of Things Past*, two Olivier Awards for Best Production including *Billy Budd*, and in 2004 was made OBE for her services to drama. From 1992, first as Co-Director, then as Director from 2000, she transferred her wealth of knowledge and experience of design for theatre and film to the Motley School at the Drury Lane Theatre in the heart of London's West End, where a project-based curriculum, taught by practising professionals, coupled with her ethos of diversity, attracted students from backgrounds as varying as architecture, engineering and archaeology, as well as those from a more traditional route of stage management and costume design.

2008
Professor Gonzalo Tassier

Born in Mexico City, Gonzalo Tassier studied philosophy at the National Autonomous University of Mexico (UNAM) School of Architecture. Despite being self-taught as a designer, Tassier's career then spanned over four decades, in which time he became Mexico's leading graphic designer. Tassier is renowned for his iconic logo and trademark designs, which include the eagle emblazoned on the shirts of the Mexican national football team. In 1995, Tassier founded the communication design agency Retorno Tassier, located in Mexico City, of which he is president; the agency has numerous Mexican and international companies as clients as well as government institutions and state organisations. He has been guest lecturer at Universidad Iberoamericana (UIA) in Mexico City and at numerous universities and colleges throughout the country. His students are on record as saying that his classes are a unique, memorable experience in their design education. As one former student has remarked "He makes you want to grab a pencil and create beautiful things. He makes you proud to be a designer".

2009
Judy Frater

Judy Frater was born in the United States and holds Masters degrees from the University of Washington and the University of Minnesota. In 1989 she became Assistant and then Associate Curator of Eastern Hemisphere Collections at the Textile Museum in Washington D.C. a position she held until 1992. Wishing to do something to preserve traditional Indian craft rather than just study it, in 1993 Frater, together with local embroiders, founded the *Kala Raksha Trust*, the first design school run largely by local artisan communities. Frater has lived in Kutch, working with artisans, for 25 years. Later she established the *Kala Raksha Textile Museum*, and founded *Kala Raksha Vidhyalaya*, a design school for traditional craftspeople. For this concept, Frater was awarded an *Ashoka Fellowship* for social entrepreneurship in 2003. Under her eight-year tenure as Director, *Kala Raksha Vidhyalaya* received international recognition for its effective approach to education of artisans. She received the Crafts Council of India Kamla Award in 2010, and the George B. Walter '36 Service to Society Award from Lawrence University in 2014.

2011
Professor Kumar Vyas
1929–2017

Born in Uganda, Kumar Vyas studied in India before training as an industrial designer at the Central School of Art and Design (now Central Saint Martins College of Design) in London. Following an invitation from the National Institute of Design (NID) to set up the Faculty of Industrial Design at their campus in Ahmedabad, Vyas returned to India and began training the first cadre of Indian industrial designers and design educators. His pioneering work at the NID helped spearhead a distinctive take on the 'Bauhaus/Ulm' approach to design. This method has become such an intrinsic part of the NID that the achievements of Kumar Vyas and his colleagues are often taken for granted, but they happened in the face of immense odds, in an environment hostile to change and loathe to surrender traditional, largely colonial, educational methods. Through his writings on design, Vyas has inspired generations of Indian designers. Building on this legacy, in 2006 Kumar Vyas helped to create the Institute of Design at the Maharashtra Institute of Technology, in Pune.

2012
Professor Ezio Manzini

Ezio Manzini began his career at the Politecnico di Milano where he studied and later went on to teach. Best known for his work in the field of design for sustainability, Manzini has specifically focused on social innovation. A testament to his innovative work is DESIS, an international network of schools of design and other design-related organisations specifically active in the field of design for social innovation and sustainability, which he founded and coordinated.

In addition Manzini has explored and promoted design in different specialities, including Design of Materials in the 1980s; Strategic Design in the 1990s (creating a Masters Degree Course in Strategic Design at the Politecnico in Milan); and since 2000 initiating specific courses in Service Design in the same institution. A prolific design researcher, writer, and educator, Manzini has received a number of prizes from prestigious Italian institutions.

2013
Professor Santiago Aránguiz Sánchez

Santiago Aránguiz Sánchez was born in Santiago de Chile. He has been widely recognised for his work in protecting Chile's cultural history and heritage of his country, and for his pioneering educational achievements in this field. This is evidenced in the museums and exhibitions he has created throughout Chile and in the archives and libraries he has established that record the cultural history and archealogical discoveries that make up the museums collections. He set up the first *Department of Museographic Design* in Chile in order to remodel and transform the dissemination of information and the organisation of cultural property in museums. In 2003, he was appointed the first Dean of the School of Design at the Universidad del Pacifico.

2014
Professor Michael Twyman

Professor Michael Twyman's long and distinguished career at the University of Reading has won him international recognition from the design community. It began with his vision for a university course which combined intellectual and practical work in what he later described as 'design for reading'. Established in 1968, it was the first course of its kind at a British university and led to the establishment of the *Department of Typography & Graphic Communication* in 1974. Michael Twyman has also contributed much to the educational programmes of international organisations including *International Council of Graphic Design and Communication Associations* (ICOGRADA) and *Association Typographique Internationale* (ATypI). His passion for embracing the wider spectrum of design in an historical context has led to the establishment of many important archives including the *Isotype Archive* and *Rickards Collection of Ephemera.* His students have described their time on his courses at Reading as 'deeply enabling' and 'inspirational'.

2015
Ravi Naidoo

Ravi Naidoo is a scientist by training with a degree in physiology and a Masters degree in Business Administration. In the wake of the collapse of apartheid, he resolved to educate the world about the design potential of the new South Africa and to educate South Africans by attracting the world's leading designers in every field to celebrate and engage in design projects. He founded *Design Indaba* in 1995 – an Annual International Design Conference, now incorporating *Design Indaba Expo* – to attract leading lights from the global design world to South Africa.

Naidoo is the Founder and Managing Director of *Interactive Africa,* a Cape Town based company that combines research and creative production to work on projects that promote South Africa. He has served on numerous international design juries and panels and his work has been recognised with awards both in South Africa and throughout the world.

2016
Margaret Calvert OBE RDI

Born in South Africa in 1936, Margaret Calvert studied illustration and printmaking at Chelsea School of Art. Calvert became Jock Kinneir's assistant, initially to work on the signage for the then-new Gatwick Airport. This was closely followed by collaboration on the radical reworking of Britain's road signs; her designs for signs on roads and motorways have stood the test of time, and have been much copied around the world. Her classic typeface 'Calvert', initially designed for the Tyne and Wear Metro, is currently used in conjunction with the 'Calvert Brody' type by the Royal College of Art. More recently she designed 'New Rail Alphabet', a digital version of 'Rail Alphabet' and 'New Transport', a digital version of the original 'Transport' lettering for the UK Government's web site.

From 1987 to 1991 she was Head of Graphic Design at the Royal College of Art, having taught there for many years, retiring as Senior Tutor in 2001. In 1976 Margaret Calvert was elected a member of the Alliance Graphique Internationale; and in 2004 an Honorary Fellow of the University of the Arts London. In 2006, she was awarded an Honorary Doctor of Letters from the University of Brighton; and in 2016 received an Honorary Doctorate from the Royal College of Art. She was elected an RSA Royal Designer for Industry in 2011, and was awarded an OBE in 2016.

2018
Professor P John Clarkson

John Clarkson began his engineering career in 1980 at the English Electric Valve Company, working on the design and production of leddicons, klystrons, travelling-wave tubes, large valves and LCD displays. He studied engineering at Trinity Hall, Cambridge, specialising in electrical sciences and focusing on the modelling and control of stepping motor systems. He then joined PA Consulting Group to work on projects ranging from the automated inspection of asthma inhalers to computer-controlled fire-fighting training. He developed a particular interest in the design process and its impact on the delivery of effective systems and satisfied clients.

In 1995 Clarkson returned to Cambridge University to embark upon a research career that would lead to ground-breaking approaches in the modelling of design processes and change propagation within complex systems. He began a long-term collaboration with Roger Coleman at the Royal College of Art to rethink mainstream design for the elderly and disabled, leading to the development of an *Inclusive Design Toolkit*, which has had far reaching impact on design education and the design of products and services around the world. His team are now developing a *Healthcare Design Toolkit* to facilitate improvements in practice.

The Sir Misha Black Award 1999–2018

**THE GLASGOW
SCHOOL:?ARt**

1999
Professor Norman McNally
Glasgow School of Art

Joining the Glasgow School of Art in 1986, Norman McNally was a major force in the development and its education there. Under his leadership, GSA's course in Product Design became recognised both nationally and across Europe as a cutting edge design programme. Students from the course won major design awards and design concept development partnerships with companies such as Nokia, Buro Happold, VW and Philips. In 1989, McNally established the joint B Eng/M Eng course in Product Design Engineering, later recognised as an exemplar. In the 1990s, McNally developed and led a new educational model, the Masters of European Design Degree, in partnership with five other institutions in Europe. In addition, McNally is a highly regarded designer, who having formed a partnership with Colin McCadden in 1978, has worked with many commercial clients in Ireland and Scotland. He represented the Scottish Office on the Design Council's education committees.

Royal College of Art
Postgraduate Art & Design

Imperial College
London

2001
Professor Roger Coleman / Dr Paul Ewing
Royal College of Art / Imperial College

Roger Coleman is well known for his work in raising the consciousness of designers and manufacturers about the issues and opportunities of designing products for an ageing population. Through both the Design Age programme at the Royal College of Art (RCA) and as Co-Director of the Helen Hamlyn Research Centre at the Royal College of Art, he was a pioneer in "the most socially worthwhile enterprise of the whole design profession". He also played a leading role in conferences and events such as the European Year of Older People (1993), which in turn led to the creation of the European Design for Ageing Network. He has researched, lectured, and published widely on the subject, from *Design Age* to *Designing for our Future Selves*.

Paul Ewing is renowned for his innovative work at the Imperial College of Science, Technology and Medicine (ICSTM), where he introduced practical design teaching to the engineering curriculum. He then expanded this approach of incorporating Art & Design project teaching into undergraduate engineering courses across the UK and internationally. His passion, knowledge and experience influenced the education of a generation of engineering students. He was also instrumental in bringing more engineering into the education of design students, "creating a new model for teaching and a new type of professional".

**UNIVERSITY OF
CAMBRIDGE**

2002
Professor Ken Wallace
Cambridge University

Through his work in the Engineering Department of Cambridge University, Ken Wallace communicated a passion for design and for the creative possibilities within professional practice to generations of engineering graduates. Wallace introduced the design of products and design theory to the curriculum, and it was his teaching approach of designing, building and testing products that led to the establishment of the Integrated Design Project – an interdisciplinary, team-working project designing autonomous robot vehicles. Wallace's research and systematic analysis of industrial design processes have had a major influence on the development of systematic engineering design methods. His achievements at Cambridge made him a leading player in the development of design in engineering courses world-wide.

The Bartlett
School of Architecture

2003
Professor Adrian Forty
Bartlett, University College London

Adrian Forty was instrumental in establishing architectural history both as an important academic discipline in its own right, and as an integral element in the architecture and design curriculum in higher education. In 1981, Forty co-founded and headed the MSc in Architectural History at the Bartlett School of Architecture, the first of its kind in Britain and soon to be internationally renowned. The course has continued to attract students from more than twenty countries. In addition, Forty's two major books *Objects of Desire* (1986) and *Words and Buildings* (2000), continue to inspire contemporary architectural and design historians as well as students and teachers. In particular, his work demonstrated the necessity of broadening the study of design and architecture to encompass ideas and methodologies derived from many other disciplines.

2004
Professor Jane McCann
University of Derby

Jane McCann has gained an international reputation as a leading authority on the subject of performance sportswear in the world of education. Having established the first and only Masters programme in Performance Sportswear Design at the University of Derby in 1995, she went on to make an outstanding contribution to the development of the field. As director of the Smart Clothes and Wearable Technologies (SCWT) Research Centre (2004–2012) at the University of South Wales, Newport, McCann attracted Joint UK Research Council funding, under the New Dynamics of Ageing programme, to lead "Design for Ageing Well" (2009–2012) with the focus on the development of a smart sports layering system for active ageing, to enhance autonomy and wellbeing. McCann continues to teach short courses in China on functional clothing and contributes to textile-oriented magazines and publications. McCann is also actively involved in responding to industry demands for reviving performance sportswear design studies at postgraduate level.

Research Centre

2006
Design Against Crime Research Centre
Central St Martins School of Art

Design Against Crime (DAC), a practice-led design research project, was founded by Lorraine Gamman in 1999 at Central Saint Martins College of Art & Design (CSM). In 2005 the DAC was recognised as a formal research centre by the University of the Arts, London. Innovative in its acknowledgment of the importance of creativity and intelligent design for the economic, cultural and social well-being of society, the DACRC has challenged students from all disciplines, including fashion, communications, industrial design, technology and cultural studies by including crime prevention as standard criteria in design briefs.

Projects undertaken by the centre have included an industry collaboration on the design of a folding – therefore more theft-proof – bicycle, furniture designs that help secure people's property in public spaces, and a number of promotional campaigns to raise awareness of patterns of crimes. Protection against crime can be, and often is, a design issue. To ensure that information is constantly updated and new developments logged, the DACRC has maintained daily contact with relevant government bodies, police and international organisations and networks

2007
Department of Industrial Design
Coventry University

The Department of Industrial Design at Coventry School of Art & Design (CSAD) has become internationally recognised as a leading centre for product design. By bringing together a wide spectrum of professionals, it has created a curriculum integrating the skills necessary to design and manufacture world-class products. This approach, applied to a wide range of taught programmes in the fields of Automotive, Product, and Transport Design, has provided a high level of excellence and the development of an international network of partners, particularly with the automotive industry, in France, Germany, Italy and USA. In addition, this helped to encourage collaborative projects, a guest visiting lecturer programme and active staff research and consultancy.

2009
Professor Anthony Dunne
Design Interactions, Royal College of Art

Anthony Dunne joined the Royal College of Art (RCA) in 1994, first as a senior research fellow in the Computer Related Design Research studio, then in 1998 as senior tutor for Design Products and in 2005 as Head of Design Interactions. As Professor of Design Interactions, he worked at the forefront of design's engagement with new branches of science, paying particular attention to developments in bio and nano technology. Through his teaching, he has sought from his students a form of critical thought, which asks the scientific community and society at large to reflect on our common future. Believing strongly that design does not mean the fabrication of 'solutions' but rather lies in the imagining of new scenarios for life, Dunne encouraged students to look at the impact the most advanced technologies have on the daily lives of nations. This is demonstrated by the types of projects Dunne's students engage in as part of the course. For example, in the Spring of 2008 Dunne's students made a significant contribution to New York's Museum of Modern Art's (MoMA) *Design and the Elastic Mind* exhibition, responsible for some of the most significant concepts in the show.

2009
Creative Research into Sound Art Practice
London College of Communication

Based at London College of Communication, Creative Research into Sound Art Practice (CRiSAP) is an organisation dedicated to the development of the emerging field of sound art and design. Through research, CRiSAP has sought to encourage the broadening and deepening of the discursive context in which sound art is practised. This has included activities in a number of different areas including engagement with relationships between sound and environment, research and dissemination of artists' practices with the spoken word, developing new creative software, and multidisciplinary and cross-cultural approaches to listening as a practice, philosophy and methodology. Students working within CRiSAP have worked collaboratively on a number of projects with other UK-based institutions such as the University of Kent Radio, the Animation department at the Royal College of Art, students at Circus Space and the London Sinfonietta. In addition, CRiSAP has been involved in international projects, such as the symposia in Zurich (2009) and Aix-en-Provence (2010) as well as an evening of performances at the Gallus Theatre in Frankfurt (2009). International projects such as these have helped develop a rewarding relationship with the Srishti School of Art, Design and Technology in Bangalore, leading to artists' residencies, workshops, and student and staff exchanges. The value of CRiSAP's work has been recognised by the British Academy, the Arts and Humanities Research Council, the Wellcome Trust and the Engineering and Physical Sciences Research Council.

2012
Manchester School of Art
Manchester Metropolitan University

Under the leadership of Professor David Crow, Manchester School of Art at Manchester Metropolitan University underwent a radical repositioning, reverting back to its original name and founding ethos of 'supporting the creative economy of the region', and with a programme to create an entirely new building and refurbish those existing sites that have fallen into disrepair. These carefully thought-out facilities reinforce the school's plans to enhance multidisciplinary and collaborative working through curriculum innovation. An innovative scheme introduced by Professor Crow and his colleagues is the experimental 'Unit X' programme. Implemented across the entire undergraduate curriculum, 'Unit X' broadens perceptions and applications of design theory by ensuring every art student takes part in an external-facing, multidisciplinary team project in each year of their study. Staff teams support this collaborative work both inside and outside the School of Art, with plans to link the staff and students at Manchester School of Art with other major institutions along what is now known as 'The Corridor', extending along Oxford Road from Manchester Central Library to the Whitworth art gallery.

2014
National Art&Design Saturday Club
The Sorrell Foundation

A model intended to support and complement the mainstream education system, the National Saturday Club aims to inspire creativity in young people, to develop their practical and career-related skills, and to encourage them towards further study and a future working in the creative sector. The National Saturday Club gives 13-16 years olds the opportunity to study art and design at their local college, university or museum. The Clubs are free and held on Saturday mornings during the academic year. This exciting programme bridges the gap between secondary and tertiary education, and gives secondary level students a broader exposure to the diverse practices of art and design, and to industry practitioners.

Club members receive up to 100 hours of specialist learning, attend masterclasses with leading art and design professionals, and take part in group events in London, including a summer exhibition of their work at Somerset House, London. The Saturday Club movement began in 2009, when The Sorrell Foundation launched the National Art&Design Saturday Club in four locations. Since then, its network has grown and flourished to encompass more than 50 Art&Design Clubs in colleges, universities and cultural institutions across the UK.

Lancaster University

2015
Professor Rachel Cooper OBE
University of Lancaster

Professor Rachel Cooper, OBE, is Distinguished Professor of Design Management and Policy at Lancaster University, and President of the Design Research Society. Professor Cooper's fields of research interest cover design management, design policy, new product development, design in the built environment, design against crime and socially responsible design. Professor Cooper, by undertaking several advisory roles to national and international universities, government and non-governmental organisations, has contributed much to the promotion of design research in the UK while retaining the confidence of the design community – often suspicious of academic research.. She is a member of the board of the Arts and Humanities Research Council and Engineering and Physical Sciences Research Council commissioning panels. In addition, she is author of several books including *The Design Agenda* (1995), *The Design Experience* (2003), *Designing Sustainable Cities* (2009), *Constructing Futures* (2010) and *A Handbook of Design Management* (2011). Cooper is currently commissioning editor for an Ashgate Series on Socially Responsible Design. She has evolved and led a significant community of researchers at Lancaster, where she supervises PhD students, in the areas of product and service design, policy and social responsibility, and management.

2016
Professor Catherine McDermott
Kingston University

Professor McDermott has pioneered new ways in which design is curated and communicated through her work in establishing the MA Curating Contemporary Design at Kingston University in partnership with the Design Museum, an innovative and already influential programme. She has been honoured for her work in academia, received a National Teaching Fellowship Award, is author of many books on contemporary design and has served on numerous national and international advisory boards. She is currently the Secretary of ICOM UK (International Committee of Museums). Latterly, she has instituted important partnerships with Chinese design educators and their students. Through her pioneering work in establishing the MA Curating Contemporary Design and through her many contributions to the understanding and appreciation of design – by teaching, publishing, curating and lecturing – Professor McDermott has built numerous bridges between design education and surrounding practices.

2016
Arts University Bournemouth

The Arts University Bournemouth grew from the Bournemouth Municipal College of Art which was the first government grant-funded school in the United Kingdom. It became the Arts Institute Bournemouth and in 2009, Arts University Bournemouth. It is now located on a purpose-built campus at Wallisdown in Poole and has grown in reputation, strength and student numbers under the direction of the present Principal and Vice-Chancellor, Professor Stuart Bartholomew. 'The Gallery' was established in 1998, winning national and international recognition and providing a major contemporary visual and performing arts resource for the University and the wider community in the South West. In March 2016, the newly-commissioned Drawing Studio, designed by Professor Sir Peter Cook, an alumnus of the Bournemouth Municipal College of Art, was opened by Zaha Hadid. The building celebrates light and provides a space to enable drawing as a focused creative activity. This building has been recognised in regional and national awards of the Royal Institute of British Architects and has been nominated for the World Architectural Federation Award. It symbolises the centrality of drawing in both art and design teaching.

2018
University of Brighton Design Archives

The University of Brighton Design Archives champions the legacy of British designers, the professional organisations that promoted and represented design, and their impact internationally. Since the mid 1990s it has made accessible a unique picture of twentieth-century British design and its role in shaping reconstruction and a democratic Britain. Both the content of the Design Archives and its innovative ethos of research-informed stewardship attract researchers and students from around the world. Its staff provoke debate and curate a dynamic and collaborative programme that links content, enquiry and practice. Principles of inclusivity and diversity underpin a collecting policy which ensures the holdings of the Design Archives inform the writing and representation of histories from various perspectives, embracing women as well as men, lesser known designers alongside the well known, and the organisations that represented them from the regional to the international. Importantly, those who visit the Design Archives are not only historians, but include artists, photographers, curators, information professionals and designers.

Ceremonies and Events

HRH Prince Philip with
Sir Misha Black in 1975

At the Awards Ceremony in 2002. In the audience are David Height,
Brian Davies, James Randle RDI, Lucienne Day RDI, Geoffrey Adams,
Santiago Calatrava, David Hamilton.

At the 2008 Awards
Ceremony. Left to right:
Tim O'Brien RDI,
Alex Moulton RDI,
Alison Chitty RDI,
Sir Christopher Frayling,
Gonzalo Tassier,
Frank Height,
Elaine Ostroff,
Ashoke Chatterjee,
Geoffrey Kirk RDI,
Mary V Mullin,
Joe Kerr.

Alison Chitty RDI (left) and Kenji Ekuan (right) awarded the Medal at the RCA in 2007 and 1995 respectively.

Sir Christopher Frayling receives the 30th Anniversary Medal from HRH Prince Philip.

Each year the recipient of the Medal is invited to give an address at the Awards Ceremony. In 2016 Margaret Calvert OBE RDI (above) gave the address and in 2008, Gonzalo Tassier (right).

The RCA Senior Common Room in readiness for the annual Awards Dinner, with Carel Weight's portrait of Sir Misha Black on display.

It has long been a tradition that students from the RCA are invited to design invitations and menus for the annual awards celebration.

Left 1999 and above 2003.

144

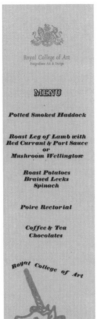

Clockwise from top left:
2000, 2016, 2008, 2006, 2007, 2005.

The Founding Bodies

Royal College of Art
Postgraduate Art & Design

The Royal College of Art is indebted to Sir Misha Black for his contribution to design; not only to generations of students who studied under his leadership between 1959 and 1975, but also to his global influence on the academic and professional advancement of both the discipline and design education. His innovation and leadership as a pedagogue are justly celebrated through the Misha Black Awards, whose recipients have propelled the advancement and contribution of design through their personal leadership in design education.

Sir Misha Black was appointed in 1959 by Sir Robin Darwin to lead the new School of Industrial Design (Engineering) at the RCA. He was already a talented and successful designer but became an extraordinary pedagogue in the field of industrial design. He was one of the first design educators to recognise that aesthetic and commercial value had to be suffused with humanism and social value, as well as technological innovation. He played a seminal role in defining the design profession and the designers' responsibility to society.

In 1975 Sir Misha Black wrote the following, which is just as applicable today:

> '...the contribution of the industrial designer to society is his creative capacity, social consciousness and human understanding, but these virtues require a technological vehicle for their expression... Industrial design is a useful art, its success or failure can only be judged in relation to its effectiveness as a social catalyst.'

Sir Misha Black set the trajectory of the College's commitment to a research-led approach to design that blended deep industry and public-sector engagement with profound reflection on the nature of the design process and the role of the designer in society. This approach is as apt today as it was at his retirement in 1975, and is manifest not only through the RCA's School of Design, but also internationally where Black's innovative thinking has inspired design education globally.

The Misha Black Awards are a celebration of his global influence, and in this 40th year the Royal College of Art is proud to celebrate Sir Misha Black's profound legacy. This legacy lives on and is a foundation for the inspiration for the RCA's continued development of design education for the twenty-first century.

Dr Paul Thompson
Vice-Chancellor
Royal College of Art

The United Kingdom has always been a country where design, and the creative industries more broadly, has flourished. The current government has recognised the creative industries as a fundamental component of the UK industrial strategy. In fields like engineering and manufacturing, it is the creative or design component or skill that marks the UK's endeavours out from other countries.

As the rise of cloud computing, data analytics, machine learning and artificial intelligence gathers pace, we begin to enter an era of man-machine partnerships. I predict that the human side of the partnership will become focussed around those most human characteristics of emotion, hunch, intuition and judgement; in essence the raw ingredients of a designer. All countries, not just the UK, will put more emphasis on designers, design thinking and design education.

The Faculty of Royal Designers for Industry comprises those that have become outstanding designers, in whatever medium or discipline they have chosen. None of us would be who we have become without excellent design education. We can only create brilliant designers with outstanding design education and educators. Quite simply, the Faculty would not exist without them.

The notion of design is expanding – it is no longer solely applied to creating beautiful physical objects but also to creating better outcomes through intangible means; services that improve our experience, or the creation of anything that enriches our lives. The future will require even more, broader and better design education. In order to get to that future, we must recognise those who so selflessly dedicate their lives to educating designers, who in turn design things or services that improve the world we live in. The Sir Misha Black Medal plays an important role in raising awareness and recognition of those educators who are truly inspirational; those that the design industry relies upon to both create new designers and attract other brilliant people to become design educators. Members of the Faculty are keen to contribute towards better design education and some are themselves also educators. All of us encourage and support the teaching of design and design thinking throughout the educational system; both formal and informal. It is with great pride that the Faculty of Royal Designers for Industry supports the Sir Misha Black Medal.

Tristram Carfrae RDI
Master of the RSA Faculty of Royal Designers for Industry

ROYAL
ACADEMY OF
ENGINEERING

Excellent design is fundamental to excellent engineering. This principle was recognised by the Fellowship of Engineering right from the time it was created in 1976, and design education became one of the first challenges that the young academy addressed. Sir Misha Black's reputation as an industrial designer of the highest calibre is widely recognised, and the Fellowship, now the Royal Academy of Engineering has been honoured to work with our partner organisations to support the Sir Misha Black Medal and Awards. Some of the world's most gifted engineering designers and architects have won these awards over the last four decades. The roll call of past winners offers a fascinating insight into late 20th and early 21st century design achievement.

Excellent engineering is only possible with a well-educated and motivated workforce, both of which depend on good teachers with the appropriate facilities and experience. During the 1980s the professional engineering institutions placed increasing importance on engineering design education, prompting many positive developments in university engineering courses. However, as financial pressures on universities rose, it became more difficult to recruit academic staff with current experience of engineering design in industry. The Fellowship appointed eight senior engineers from industry as the first Visiting Professors in the Principles of Engineering Design in 1989. Since then, over 200 leading industrial engineers have shared their knowledge and experience with engineering undergraduates through this innovative scheme.

The Visiting Professors aimed to ensure that modern industrial practice, both technical and managerial, would be reflected in both teaching and project work in UK universities. As an added benefit, they also provided a conduit for a productive exchange of ideas and research back into industry, often forming the foundation for long-term collaborations between academia and business.

More recently, the Royal Academy of Engineering expanded and diversified the scheme to include engineering design for sustainable development and integrated systems engineering. Learning from the scheme informed our extensive current programme of Visiting Professorships across all areas of engineering.

The role of design engineers in industry is changing rapidly, thanks to the development of powerful computational design tools, virtual reality and advanced manufacturing techniques. There is now a much greater emphasis on understanding the impact of engineering on the environment and society and a responsibility to consider impacts over the whole lifecycle of a product. Future design education must continue to embody these aspects while still maintaining the rigour required of good engineering, and Sir Misha Black's design legacy is sure to play a lasting role in achieving this.

Professor Dame Ann Dowling OM DBE FREng FRS
President
Royal Academy of Engineering

Britain can be proud of its record in developing a pattern of design education over the past 180 years, which has resulted in the spread of art and design colleges (now mainly incorporated into universities) throughout the country and covering all design disciplines. This initiative, backed by Government funds, has provided a source of designers for industry and commerce unmatched by other industrialised nations.

When the Design and Industries Association came to be founded in 1915, with the aim of bringing together designers and industrialists, it was natural that education, in its widest sense, should be seen as a principal channel for its work. Through the organisation of exhibitions, either on its own account or in conjunction with other organisations, together with publications, lectures and discussion meetings, the Association has focused on encouraging acceptance of the importance of design with a view ultimately to influencing the general public, as consumers. Its pioneering work in these fields was influential in the formation of the Society of Industrial Artists and Designers in 1930 and the Council of Industrial Design (later, Design Council) in 1944.

In 1965, primarily to underpin this work, an educational trust was established with charitable status to raise funds and make grants for scholarships and awards and to support research projects. The DIA Trust has formed the main link between the Association and the Sir Misha Black Awards.

The DIA fully supported the establishment of the Medal as a memorial to Sir Misha Black, who had been involved with the Association since the 1930s and was President of the DIA in 1974-76. It was entirely appropriate that this should recognise distinction in design education and that it was widened in scope in 1998 by the introduction of the Award for Innovation in Design Education. It is noteworthy that the Awards remain, after 40 years, the only recognition for achievement in this field, internationally and covering all aspects of design.

The first 40 years of the Sir Misha Black Awards have witnessed a wider acceptance of the importance of design in industry in the UK and an upgrade in the level and recognition of design education. It would be encouraging to credit the Awards with playing a part in bringing this about through their role in raising the profile of design education.

It is essential that this work is continued, if design is to maintain – and preferably increase – its influence and standing in British commercial life. Economic demands, including price cutting, may exert contrary pressures, but design, with developing technologies, has an important contribution to make here as well. To justify and sustain the reputation of UK design, it is vital that our designers should be properly trained so that they may continue to match, if not surpass, the creativity and skill of any in the world.

Geoffrey Adams

Design & Industries Association

The Sir Misha Black Awards

Lithograph of Sir Misha Black by Gordon Lawson, 1975

History and Development

Geoffrey Adams
Design & Industries Association

When Professor Sir Misha Black OBE RDI PPSIAD died in August 1977, it came as a profound shock to his colleagues in the design profession. Sir Misha had been associated with a number of 'firsts': with Milner Gray he had established the first multi-disciplinary body of professional designers in the world, the Society of Industrial Artists and Designers (SIAD); he was the first Professor of Industrial Design at the Royal College of Art (RCA); he was closely involved in the formation of the International Council of Societies of Industrial Design (ICSID); and he was the first person to be knighted for services to industrial design. He died young, and unexpectedly.

After his death, the SIAD, which had a long history of involvement in design education in the UK, set up a working party of design organisations with which Sir Misha had been associated to decide on a suitable memorial.

The members of the working party were:

> **Robert Wetmore**, President, SIAD
> *– Misha Black had been President in 1954–56*
> **Raymond Plummer**, Hon Director, Design & Industries Association
> *– Misha Black had been President from 1974–76*
> **Lord Esher**, Rector, and later his successor **Professor Richard Guyatt**, Royal College of Art
> *– Misha Black was Professor of Industrial Design there from 1959–75,*
>   *subsequently Emeritus Professor*
> **Neville Ward**, Master of the RSA Faculty of Royal Designers for Industry
> *– Misha Black had been Master of the Faculty from 1973–74*
> **Leslie Julius**, SIAD
> The administration was provided by the SIAD

At its first meeting, on 3 February 1978, the working party decided that the memorial should take the form of a medal bearing Sir Misha's head, to be awarded for work of particular significance in design education – in recognition of his long service and personal distinction in this field. It was not intended that the medal be given in perpetuity, but that it should last for the living memory of his friends, perhaps a period of some 25 years. The medal, to be awarded biennially (which remained broadly the position until it became an annual event in 1995), was to be open to potential recipients from the UK and worldwide. 'Worldwide' had been important to Sir Misha Black.

Michael Rizzello FSIAD was commissioned to model the portrait from a photograph chosen by Lady Black, who had approved the proposal for the form of the award. The name of the Medallist, with the year, is inscribed on the outer edge. Initially 12 copies were cast in bronze by the Royal Mint, supervised by Michael Rizzello and Milner Gray – Sir Misha's partner in Industrial Design Unit – who designed the embossed lettering. In 1991 a presentation case, in the form of a wooden box, was designed at the RCA following a competition between first year postgraduate students; more recently the boxes have been made from walnut by Dorset woodturner, David Hirst.

The first recipient was Sir William Coldstream CBE and the Duke of Edinburgh, Patron of the SIAD, agreed to present the medal at a small ceremony which took place in the Chinese Dining Room at Buckingham Palace on 6 December 1978. Prince Philip accepted a replica of the medal, in a Perspex casing, from Richard Negus, President of the SIAD.

During its first 15 years, the organisational pattern for the Awards broadly followed the arrangements made in 1978 (albeit without the participation of Prince Philip). It had originally been hoped that Medallists would come to London to receive their medal, and deliver a paper at the ceremony. However, an appeal for funds in 1978/79 did not raise enough to pay for the commissioning of a paper or to cover travel expenses from abroad. So a procedure was devised to present the medal either at an existing SIAD event or, for an overseas recipient, in the their home country. Medallists were not expected to prepare or read a paper, unless they offered to.

The administration of the Awards continued to be provided by the SIAD, which changed its name to the Chartered Society of Designers (CSD) in 1987, consulting with the founding bodies over the selection of the recipient and the presentation of the medal. After a period of organisational disruption at the CSD, the administration of the Awards was transferred to the RCA in March 1993, when the College undertook to provide the medal Committee with administrative and secretarial support until 2012 (open to renewal) and to house the Committee's archive in the RCA Library. Ms Graca Tavares de Almeida, Assistant Registrar of the College, joined the Committee as Administrator in 1995.

The new arrangements were made possible through the good offices of Professor Frank Height who was Sir Misha Black's successor at the RCA. He served on the Committee as representative of the CSD and later the College of Medallists and remained a Special Adviser to the Committee until his death. A wise, long-serving, and generous catalyst, anchoring the Committee.

With the transfer of the administration, the Committee was placed on a more formal basis, while still comprising representatives of the founding bodies. Its members were: Professor David Hamilton (RCA), Ms Mary V Mullin (DIA), Mrs Lucienne Day (RSA, Faculty of RDIs), and Professor Frank Height (CSD). Professor Hamilton, Head of the Faculty of Art and Design at the RCA, who had joined the Committee as the College representative in 1980 (replacing Professor Guyatt), was appointed Chairman in 1993.

The following year the Committee's membership was widened to include the Royal Academy of Engineering, represented by Professor James Randle, in recognition of the close relationship between the design and engineering professions and especially the direct working link between the RCA and neighbouring Imperial College, University of London – a link for which Misha Black had campaigned in the mid-1970s.

In another substantial development, reflecting developments in design education which had happened over the previous 20 years – and its increasing prominence – in 1998 the Committee established a second Award for Innovation in Design Education. This was intended to mark the achievements of individuals in mid-career, or of UK design institutions. The first Award was made in 1999.

This Award, which takes the form of a certificate, is open to all design disciplines in the UK, including Industrial, Product, Engineering, Craft, Communications, Information Technology, Interaction and Design Management. In 2001 the Committee decided to broaden the brief to encompass a design educator, an institution, a department, a college or a particular exhibition, publication or website contributing to the development of design education through innovative teaching, course design or the relationship between education and professional design practice.

In 2003 the College of Medallists was formed to provide a mechanism for honouring past recipients of the medal. Professor Frank Height was appointed to represent the College on the Committee serving until 2010, and continuing as Special Adviser until his death in 2013. He was succeeded by Professor Sir Christopher Frayling.

Financing an annual award posed a major challenge to the Committee, particularly when, from the mid-1990s, a pattern for the presentation was established which involved a talk by the Medallist, followed by a dinner. Annual subscriptions from the founding bodies funded the Committee's general expenses, but the cost of the annual presentations has been met over a number of years by sponsors, including the Allied Irish Bank and the John Lewis Partnership. The Irish, Mexican and Chilean Embassies in London provided sponsorship in kind in years when their nationals received awards.

Later the Committee started to look for sponsorship from industry and commerce to provide a more stable and dependable financial basis for the future by establishing a category of supporting Patrons. These currently are: IDEO, Rolls Royce, Ove Arup and Design & Industries Association Trust.

Presentation ceremonies normally take place at the RCA and are public occasions. When Alex Moulton CBE RDI was awarded the medal in 1997, the event was held at the Royal Academy of Engineering and attracted a large attendance from aficionados of Moulton Bicycles to hear his talk. Prince Philip attended the presentation of the medal to Professor Sir Christopher Frayling in 2003 to mark the 25th anniversary of the award. Medallists are invited to give a presentation of their work and of their thoughts on design education, indicating how they feel their work has influenced or inspired contemporary teaching and learning. This tradition continues, forming a link between Sir Misha Black's career, past recipients of the Medal and Award, and the future.

Awards Process

Mary V Mullin introducing the Awards Ceremony at the RCA in 2016

How the Medal is Given

Mary V Mullin
Chairman of the Sir Misha Black Awards Committee

The forty years since the first Misha Black Medal was presented in Buckingham Palace in 1978 might be likened to a relay race. The distinguished representatives of the organisations in which Sir Misha had played a leading role, his colleagues, would perhaps be surprised that a 40th Anniversary Medal would be struck and presented; surprised that their successors – to whom they passed the baton of trust – have ensured that the race is far from over.

Learned Societies and Institutions may decree and authorise but it is the dedicated individuals within organisations who carry the burden. They serve out of a firm belief in the importance of design education. They know that the end result – trained, dedicated designers working throughout society – will be for the benefit of the individual, the community, the economy and the wider world. Managing voluntary effort is the hardest management job in the world: there are no sanctions. But with the Misha Black Committee, there was never need. The individuals who have represented the Founding Bodies since 1978 are named over the page and it is entirely due to their spirit of collective collaboration and enormous goodwill that this milestone has been achieved. Their debates are forceful, rigorous though always respectful; opinions are always challenged. The work of the Committee has grown in scope and breadth over the years. It should be noted and acknowledged that since its inception each representative on the Committee has contributed their time and expertise on an entirely voluntary basis.

Nowadays nominations for the Medal are sought throughout the world and, since 2009, across the United Kingdom for the Awards for Innovation. Invitations, to submit names of possible candidates, are sent to the network of distinguished Fellows of the Founding Bodies, professors and academics, industrialists, National and International Design Organisations and any interested person may complete a nomination form. These forms are designed to allow equal and fair assessment on similar grounds. The final decision on the awards rests with the Committee.

Medallists have come from five continents and illustrate the development of design education throughout the world – a cause for which Sir Misha campaigned. His work and that of his colleagues at the Royal College of Art inspired others. Many of the early teachers in countries where design education was just beginning had themselves been students of Sir Misha. Innovation in design education is now happening everywhere and the Committee knows the importance of recognising this constant striving for new ways to apply design principles and train and inspire bright young students.

The Committee appreciates all those who have supported their efforts and shared their belief that dedicated, design teachers do not get the recognition they deserve. My thanks are due to my colleagues who are a constant source of inspiration and encouragement. It has been an honour and a privilege to work with them and for us all to meet and know those who have been recognised – *at last!* – for their distinguished services to design education.

The Awards Committee

Original working party 1977-78

Robert Wetmore, President, SIAD
Raymond Plummer, Hon Director, Design & Industries Association
Lord Esher, Rector, Royal College of Art, *and later his successor*
Professor Richard Guyatt, Rector, Royal College of Art
Neville Ward, Master of the RSA Faculty of Royal Designers for Industry
Leslie Julius, SIAD

Administration provided by the SIAD
Geoffrey Adams, Secretary and CEO, SIAD

Past Committee members

1979–2003 Professor Frank Height (Chartered Society of Designers)
1993–2003 Professor David Hamilton (Royal College of Art), Chairman
1993–2007 Lucienne Day RDI (RSA Faculty of Royal Designers for Industry)
1994–2015 Professor James Randle RDI FREng (Royal Academy of Engineering)
2002–2016 Joe Kerr (Royal College of Art)
2003–2010 Professor Frank Height (College of Medallists)
2007–2011 Timothy O'Brien RDI (RSA Faculty of Royal Designers for Industry)

1979–2018 Administration provided by the RCA

Present Committee

1993–   Mary V. Mullin (Design & Industries Association), Chairman from 2003
2013–   Professor Sir Christopher Frayling (College of Medallists)
2011–   Professor Malcolm Garrett RDI (RSA Faculty of Royal Designers for Industry)
2016–   Professor Geoffrey Kirk RDI FREng (Royal Academy of Engineering)
2017–   Dr Nick de Leon (Royal College of Art)

Special Advisers

2010–2013 Professor Frank Height (College of Medallists)
2015–   Professor James Randle RDI FREng (Royal Academy of Engineering)

Acknowledgements

Dedicated to the memory of Sir Misha Black

Acknowledgements

HRH The Duke of Edinburgh for graciously writing the foreword.

The Royal Commission for the Exhibition of 1851 for helping to sponsor this publication.

The Founding Bodies for contributions over the years.

Graça Tavares de Almeida (RCA Assistant Registrar 1995–2010) for dedication to the Administration of the Awards.

The Black Papers on Design, edited by Avril Blake in 1983, and published on behalf of the Royal Designers for Industry, for collecting Sir Misha Black's writings and giving them wider circulation.

Patrons

Design & Industries Association Education Trust, IDEO, Ove Arup, Rolls-Royce

Current and past sponsors

Allied Irish Bank, Apple Computer, Belmond, The British Cement Corporation, The Bugatti Trust, Chilean Embassy, John Lewis Partnership, Mexican Embassy

Thanks

Oliver Black; Jane Crowther, G . F Smith; Neil Parkinson, RCA Archives & Collections

Thank you especially to all the contributors

The contributions of individuals to the teaching of design at all levels are still not adequately valued. They have demonstrated, through their examples, how design can create value out of technology, how design can energise industry, and how design can be a satisfying career.

HRH The Prince Philip, Duke of Edinburgh